MathFlare

Name: ________________________

Class: ___________

Teacher: ________________________

Introduction

As parents and educators, we recognize the pivotal role mathematics plays in shaping a child's academic journey and future success. Yet, the path to mathematical proficiency can often seem daunting, fraught with challenges and complexities. That's where the transformative power of MathFlare Workbooks shine through, illuminating the way forward with clarity, precision, and purpose.

Introducing MathFlare Workbooks – a beacon of guidance, a testament to excellence, and a catalyst for achievement. Crafted with meticulous care and expertise, MathFlare Workbooks stand as paragons of educational excellence, designed to nurture young minds, ignite a passion for learning, and develop a deep-rooted understanding of mathematical concepts.

Picture this: your child eagerly delves into the pages of Mathflare Workbook, greeted by a step-by-step guide illuminated with vivid examples that demystify complex mathematical concepts. With each turn of the page, they embark on a journey of discovery, encountering thoughtfully curated practice questions that reinforce learning and hone problem-solving skills. And when they unveil the answers to those very questions, a sense of accomplishment blossoms within them – a tangible reward for their hard work and dedication.

But MathFlare Workbooks are more than just tools for learning; they are pathways to comprehension, fostering a deep-seated understanding of mathematical concepts through a sequential, logical flow. From fundamental principles to advanced problem-solving strategies, every chapter builds upon the last, ensuring a robust foundation upon which future knowledge can be constructed.

As parents, we yearn for nothing more than to see our children thrive, to witness the spark of inspiration ignited within them as they conquer academic challenges with confidence and poise. MathFlare Workbooks serve as partners in this noble endeavor, offering not just practice questions, but the keys to unlocking a world of opportunity.

And for teachers, MathFlare Workbooks stand as invaluable allies in the quest to cultivate mathematical proficiency in the classroom. With answers readily available, instructors can focus on guiding and nurturing their students, confident in the knowledge that MathFlare Workbooks provide a solid framework upon which to build.

In the pages of MathFlare Workbooks, we find not just the promise of academic excellence, but the seeds of a brighter tomorrow. So let us embrace the power of mathematics, let us champion the journey of learning, and let us pave the way for a generation of young minds poised to shape the world. With MathFlare Workbooks as our guide, the possibilities are infinite, and the future, bright.

Table of Contents

MathFlare
MATH
WORKBOOK
Grade 2
Step by Step Guide
and Essential Practice
with Answers
Addition
Subtraction
Multiplication
Place Value and
Expanded
Notations
Geometry
MathFlare Publishing

MathFlare
MATH
WORKBOOK
Grade 2-3
Step by Step Guide
and Essential Practice
with Answers
Addition
Subtraction
Multiplication
and Division
Place Value and
Expanded
Notations
Geometry
MathFlare Publishing

MathFlare
MATH
WORKBOOK
Grade 3
Step by Step Guide
and Essential Practice
with Answers
Multiplication
and Division
Decimals
Place Value and
Expanded
Notations
Fractions
and Geometry
MathFlare Publishing

MathFlare
MATH
WORKBOOK
Grade 1
Step by Step Guide
and Essential Practice
with Answers
Counting and
Numbers
Addition and
Subtraction
Place Value and
Expanded
Notations
Understanding
Time
MathFlare Publishing

MathFlare
MATH
WORKBOOK
Grade 1-2
Step by Step Guide
and Essential Practice
with Answers
Counting and
Numbers
Addition and
Subtraction
Place Value and
Expanded
Notations
Understanding
Time
MathFlare Publishing

MathFlare
MATH
WORKBOOK
Grade 3-4
Step by Step Guide
and Essential Practice
with Answers
Addition
Subtraction
Multiplication
Division
Place Value and
Expanded
Notations
Fractions
and Geometry
MathFlare Publishing

MathFlare
MATH
WORKBOOK
Grade 4
Step by Step Guide
and Essential Practice
with Answers
Addition
Subtraction
Multiplication
Division
Place Value and
Expanded
Notations
Fractions
and Geometry
MathFlare Publishing

MathFlare
MATH
WORKBOOK
Grade 4-5
Step by Step Guide
and Essential Practice
with Answers
Multiplication
Division
Place Value and
Expanded
Notations
Fractions
and Geometry
Unit
Conversion
MathFlare Publishing

MathFlare
MATH WORKBOOK
Grade 5
Step by Step Guide and Essential Practice with Answers
Multiplication Division
Place Value and Expanded Notations
Fractions and Geometry
Unit Conversion
MathFlare Publishing

MathFlare
MATH WORKBOOK
Grade 5-6
Step by Step Guide and Essential Practice with Answers
Multiplication Division
Place Value and Expanded Notations
Fractions and Geometry
Units and Statistics
MathFlare Publishing

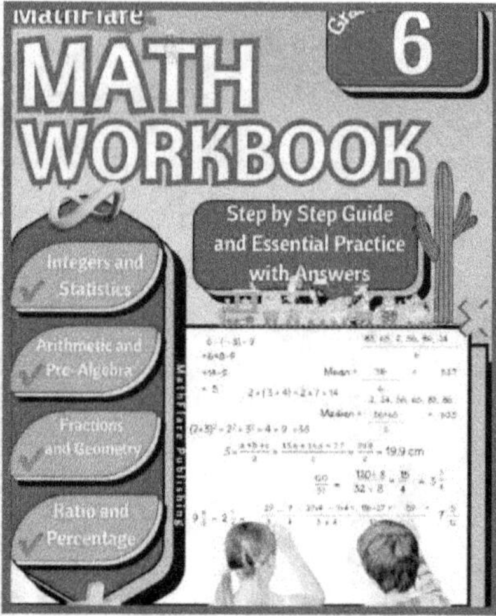
MathFlare
MATH WORKBOOK
Grade 6
Step by Step Guide and Essential Practice with Answers
Integers and Statistics
Arithmetic and Pre-Algebra
Fractions and Geometry
Ratio and Percentage
MathFlare Publishing

MathFlare
MATH WORKBOOK
Grade 6-7
Step by Step Guide and Essential Practice with Answers
Arithmetic and Pre-Algebra
Ratio, Percent Proportion
Geometry
Statistics
MathFlare Publishing

MathFlare
MATH WORKBOOK
Grade 7
Step by Step Guide and Essential Practice with Answers
Pre-Algebra
Ratio, Percent Proportion
Geometry
Statistics
MathFlare Publishing

MathFlare
MATH WORKBOOK
Grade 7-8
Step by Step Guide and Essential Practice with Answers
Pre-Algebra
Ratio, Percent Proportion
Geometry and Cartesian Plane
Statistics
MathFlare Publishing

MathFlare
MATH WORKBOOK
Grade 8-9
Step by Step Guide and Essential Practice with Answers
Pre-Algebra
Ratio, Proportion and Percentage
Linear Equations
Geometry and Cartesian Plane
MathFlare Publishing

MathFlare
MATH WORKBOOK
Grade 8
Step by Step Guide and Essential Practice with Answers
Pre-Algebra
Percentage
Linear Equations
Geometry
MathFlare Publishing

Operations with Whole Numbers

Positive and negative integers are whole numbers that can represent quantities greater than zero and less than zero, respectively.

Positive Integers: Positive integers are whole numbers greater than zero. They are denoted by the numbers 1,2,3,4...

Negative Integers: Negative integers are whole numbers less than zero. They are denoted by placing a negative sign ("-") before the numbers, such as −1,−2,−3,−4,...

The positive integers are used to represent the number of objects, scores, etc. whereas the negative integers can be used to represent debt, losses, temperatures below freezing points, etc.

Let's solve some problems:

1. $6 - (-8) - 9$

- Start by simplifying within the parentheses:

$$-(-8) \text{ becomes } 8.$$

- Rewrite the expression with the simplified part:

$$6 + 8 - 9.$$

- Now perform addition and subtraction from left to right:

$$6 + 8 = 14, \text{ then } 14 - 9 = 5$$

2. $(-5) - (-3) + 10$

$$(-5) + 3 + 10$$

$$(-5) + 3 = -2, \text{ then } -2 + 10 = 8$$

Order of Operations (PEMDAS)

The order of operations, often remembered by the acronym PEMDAS, stands for:

- **Parentheses**: Perform operations inside parentheses first.
- **Exponents**: Evaluate exponents (powers and roots) next.
- **Multiplication and Division**: Perform multiplication and division from left to right.
- **Addition and Subtraction**: Perform addition and subtraction from left to right.

The order of operations helps to clarify which operations should be performed first in a mathematical expression to ensure consistent and accurate results.

- **Parentheses**: Evaluate expressions within parentheses first. If there are nested parentheses, start with the innermost ones and work your way out.

    1. Example: $2 \times (3 + 4) = 2 \times 7 = 14$

- **Exponents**: Evaluate expressions with exponents (powers and roots) next.

    1. Example: $2^3 + 4 = 8 + 4 = 12$

- **Multiplication and Division**: Perform multiplication and division from left to right.

    1. Example: $2 \times 3 + 4 = 6 + 4 = 10$

    2. Example: $6 \div 2 \times 3 = 3 \times 3 = 9$

- **Addition and Subtraction**: Perform addition and subtraction from left to right.

    1. Example: $2 + 3 \times 4 = 2 + 12 = 14$

    2. Example: $10 - 4 \div 2 = 10 - 2 = 8$

Exponents and Roots

Exponents

An exponent tells us how many times a number (called the base) is multiplied by itself. It is written as a superscript to the right of the base number. For example, in 2^3, 2 is the base and 3 is the exponent.

Rules:

1. **Product Rule**: When multiplying powers with the same base, add the exponents.

$$a^m \times a^n = a^{m+n}$$

For example:

$$2^3 = 2 \times 2 \times 2 = 8$$

$$3^2 \times 3^4 = 3^{2+4} = 3^6 = 3 \times 3 \times 3 \times 3 \times 3 \times 3 = 729$$

2. **Quotient Rule**: When dividing powers with the same base, subtract the exponents.

$$a^m \div a^n = a^{m-n}$$

For example:

$$5^3 \div 5^2 = 5^{3-2} = 5^1 = 5$$

3. **Power of a Power Rule**: When raising a power to another power, multiply the exponents.

$$(a^m)^n = a^{mn}$$

For example:

$$(2^2)^3 = 2^{2 \times 3} = 2^6 = 64$$

4. **Power of a Product Rule**: When raising a product to a power, distribute the power to each factor.

$$(ab)^n = a^n \times b^n$$

For example:

$$(2 \times 3)^2 = 2^2 \times 3^2 = 4 \times 9 = 36$$

5. **Power of a Quotient Rule**: When raising a quotient to a power, distribute the power to the numerator and denominator separately.

$$\left(\frac{a}{b}\right)^n = \frac{a^n}{b^n}$$

For example:

$$\left(\frac{4}{2}\right)^3 = \frac{4^3}{2^3} = \frac{64}{8} = 8$$

6. **Zero Exponent Rule**: Any nonzero number raised to the power of zero equals 11.

$$a^0 = 1$$

For example:

$$7^0 = 1$$

7. **Negative Exponent Rule**: A negative exponent means the reciprocal of the base raised to the positive exponent.

$$a^{-n} = \frac{1}{a^n}$$

For example:

$$2^{-3} = \frac{1}{2^3} = \frac{1}{8}$$

To evaluate expressions with exponents, we can use:

- **Repeated Multiplication**: Perform the multiplication indicated by the exponent.

- **Using the Rules of Exponents**: Apply the appropriate rule to simplify expressions involving exponents.

Square Roots

The square root of a number is a value that, when multiplied by itself, gives the original number. It's denoted by the symbol $\sqrt{}$.

For example, the square root of 9 is 3 because 3 * 3 = 9.

Cube Roots

The cube root of a number is a value that, when multiplied by itself twice, gives the original number. It's denoted by the symbol $\sqrt[3]{}$.

For example, the cube root of 8 is 2 because 2 * 2 * 2 = 8.

<u>Evaluate Expressions</u>

Evaluating expressions involves substituting given values for variables in an expression and then performing the indicated operations to find the result.

For example: Let's evaluate $4x - 10$, when $x = 3$:

Step 1: Substitute the given value for the variable:

Replace every occurrence of x in the expression $4x - 10$ with the given value, which is 3:

$$= 4(3) - 10$$

Step 2: Perform the operations:

Perform the indicated operations according to the order of operations (PEMDAS - Parentheses, Exponents, Multiplication and Division, Addition and Subtraction):

$$= 4 \times 3 - 10$$

Step 3: Simplify:

Calculate the result:

$$12 - 10 = 2$$

<u>Solving Equations (One Step)</u>

Solving one-step equations involves performing a single operation to isolate the variable and find its value.

Let's solve an equation step by step: $16 + x = 31$

1. **Identify the Goal:**

     The goal is to isolate the variable x on one side of the equation.

2. **Simplify the Equation**: Combine like terms on both sides of the equation, if necessary.

   The equation is already simplified.

3. **Undo Addition or Subtraction**: If there's addition or subtraction involving the variable, undo it by performing the opposite operation on both sides of the equation.

   Since x is being added to 16, we'll undo this operation by subtracting 16 from both sides of the equation:

   $$16 + x - 16 = 31 - 16$$

4. **Isolate the Variable**: Ensure that the variable is alone on one side of the equation.

   $$x = 15$$

5. **Check Your Solution**: Substitute the value of x back into the original equation to verify that it satisfies the equation.

   $$16 + 15 = 31$$

   $$31 = 31$$

   The equation is balanced, so the solution.

Equations (Two Sides)

A two-sided equation is an equation where both sides have expressions with variables and constants. The goal when solving a two-sided equation is to find the value of the variable that makes both sides equal.

For example: Let's solve an equation:

$$9 + 8x + 8 = 64 + x + 2$$

- **Combine Like Terms:** Simplify each side of the equation by combining like terms (terms with the same variable or constants).

$$9 + 8x + 8 = 64 + x + 2$$

$$17 + 8x = 66 + x$$

- **Isolate the Variable:** Use inverse operations to isolate the variable on one side of the equation.

subtract x from both sides:

$$17 + 8x - x = 66 + x - x$$

$$17 + 7x = 66$$

subtracting 17 from both sides:

$$17 - 17 + 7x = 66 - 17$$

$$7x = 49$$

divide both sides by 7:

$$\frac{7x}{7} = \frac{49}{7} = x = 7$$

- **Check Solution:** Once you find the solution, substitute it back into the original equation to ensure it makes the equation true.

Substitute $x = 7$ back into the original equation:

$$9 + 8(7) + 8 = 64 + 7 + 2$$

$$9 + 56 + 8 = 64 + 7 + 2$$

$$73 = 73$$

Solving Inequalities

Inequalities are mathematical expressions that compare the relative sizes of two values. They are used to express relationships where one quantity is:

- "<" (less than),
- ">" (greater than),
- "<=" (less than or equal to),
- ">=" (greater than or equal to),
- and "≠" (not equal to) another quantity.

For example:

$$y + -10 \leq -8$$

To isolate y, we need to get rid of the constant term −10. Since −10 is being subtracted from y, we can undo this operation by adding 10 to both sides of the inequality:

Name:_____________________ Date: ____________

Operations with Whole Numbers
Evaluate Expressions.

1. $(2)(1)(-10) =$

2. $7 \div -2 =$

3. $-10 \div 2 =$

4. $(9)(-9)(-10) =$

5. $-5 \div -9 =$

6. $(10)(3)(-7) =$

7. $(-8) + (-10) + 1 =$

8. $9 \div -2 =$

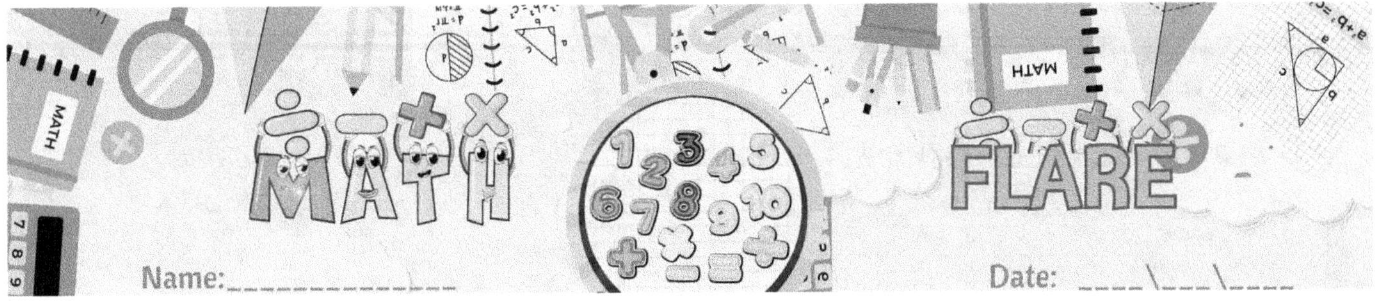

Name:________________   Date: _______________

9. $(-6) + 10 - (-3) =$

10. $(-7) - 9 - (-5) =$

11. $9 - (-3) - 6 =$

12. $10 - 5 - (-9) =$

13. $8 + (-2) - (-10) =$

14. $(-5) + (-2) + 5 =$

15. $(7)(3)(4) =$

16. $(2)(10) =$

17. $(-1)(-1)(-2) =$

18. $(-5) + 3 - (-1) =$

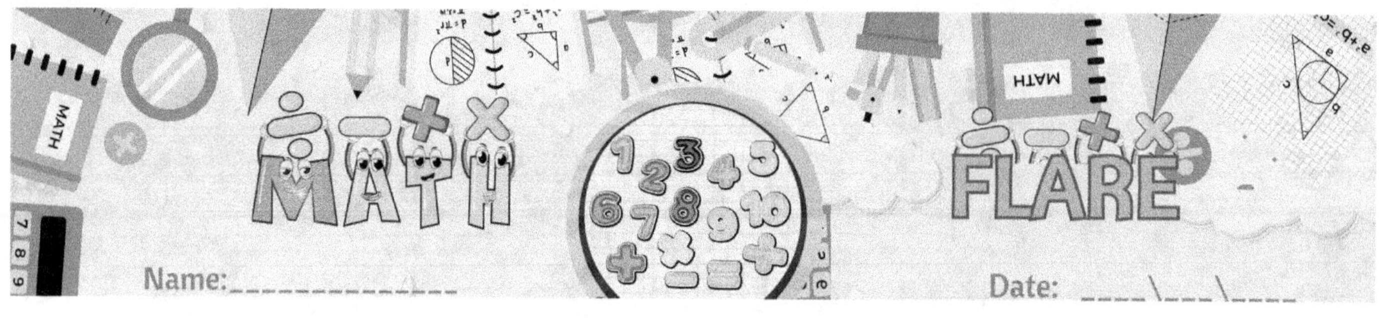

19. $(-10) - 1 - 4 =$

20. $(-9)(-2)(7) =$

21. $-3 \div 8 =$

22. $-3 \div -8 =$

23. $8 + (-2) + 10 =$

24. $4 + (-9) + (-5) =$

25. $7 + (-1 + 8) =$

26. $(-4)(-2)(7) =$

27. $(5)(-4)(6) =$

28. $(9)(-5)(-1) =$

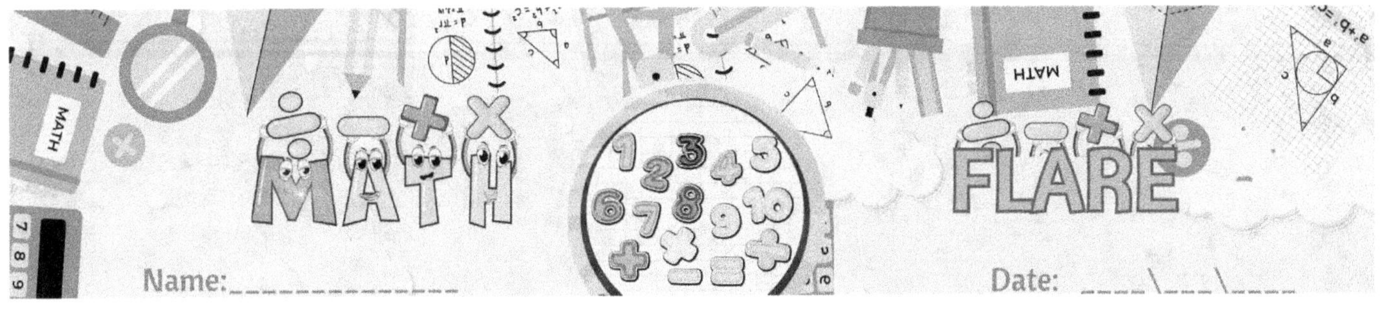

29. $(-3) + (-6) + 8 =$

30. $1 + (-6) + (-3) =$

31. $(-6)(-9) =$

32. $2 - 10 - (-6) =$

33. $(-6) + 7 - (-7) =$

34. $(-9) - 8 - 9 =$

35. $-(-2)(-5) =$

36. $(-8) + 1 - 6 =$

37. $5 \div 1 =$

38. $(7)(9)(-9) =$

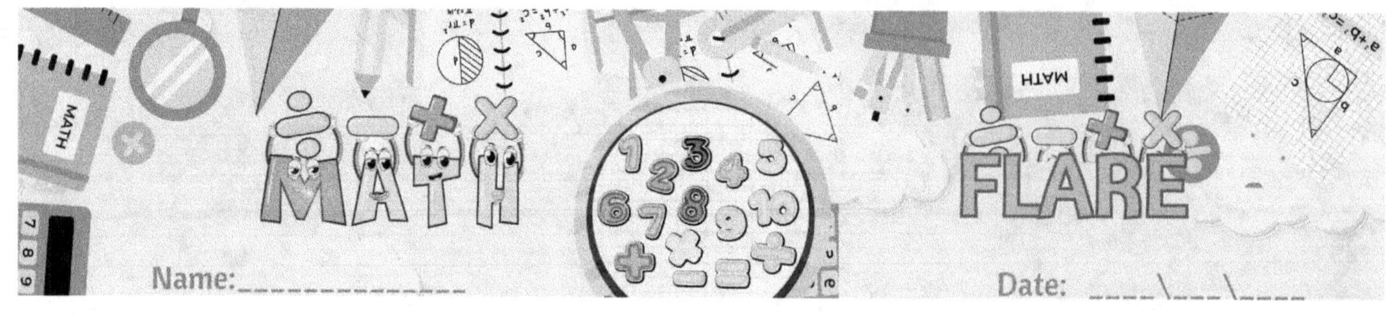

39. $-(-4)(7) =$

40. $(-10) - 4 + 4 =$

41. $3 - 3 - (-6) =$

42. $-8 \div -1 =$

43. $(-8) - 6 + 7 =$

44. $8 \div 1 =$

45. $4 + (-8) + 6 =$

46. $(-3)(-7) =$

47. $(5)(-8)(-7) =$

48. $(6)(4)(-5) =$

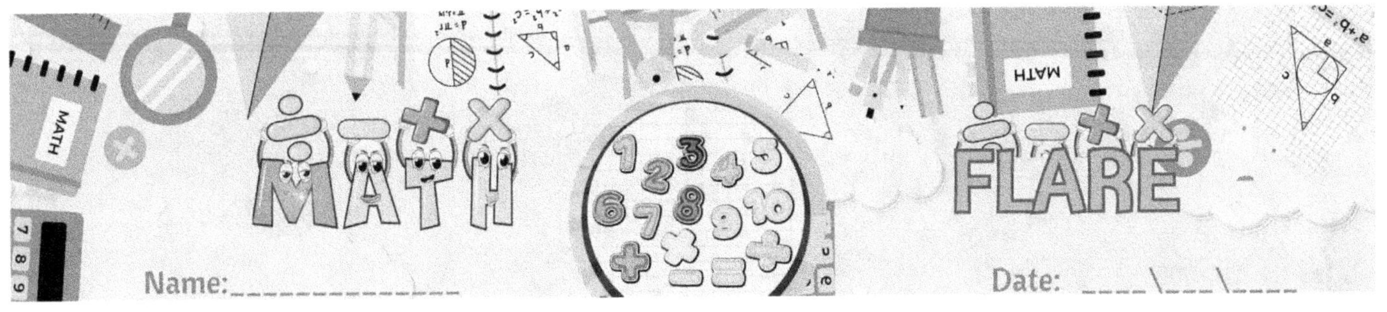

49. $(7)(10)(-7) =$

50. $-2 \div 7 =$

51. $(4)(7)(-4) =$

52. $(-3)(3) =$

53. $-2 \div 6 =$

54. $(2)(4)(-5) =$

55. $(2)(-2)(8) =$

56. $1 \div -6 =$

57. $-(-8)(-1) =$

58. $(1)(2)(8) =$

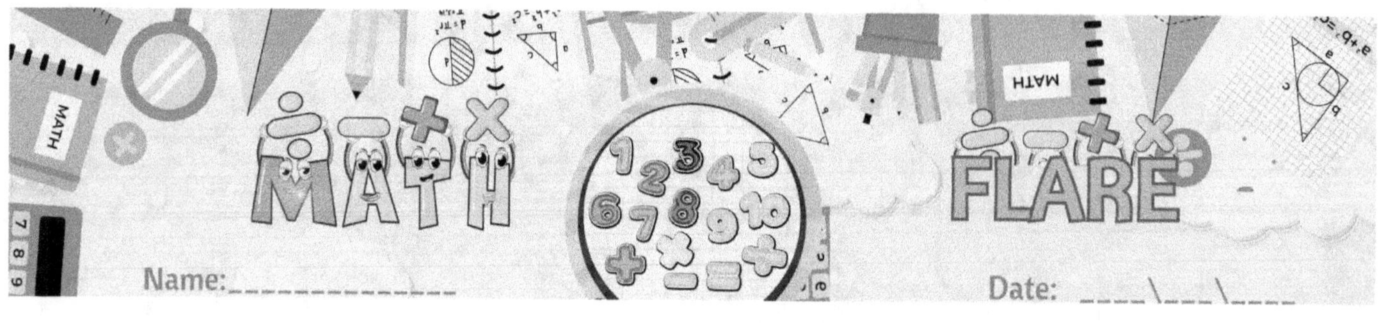

59. $(-5)(-4)(-3) =$

60. $5 + (-6) - (-10) =$

61. $4 \div 1 =$

62. $10 + (-6) + 3 =$

63. $(-10)(7)(4) =$

64. $-4 \div -10 =$

65. $(-4)(-5) =$

66. $(9)(2)(2) =$

67. $(5)(-9)(3) =$

68. $(-4) - 7 + (-10) =$

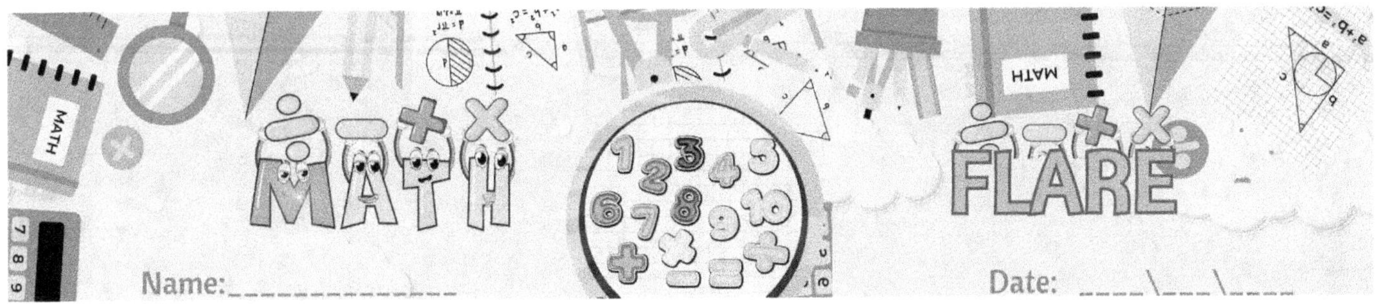

Exponents

Convert the values.

69. $13^{-2} =$ _______________

70. $18^{-2} =$ _______________

71. $15^{-3} =$ _______________

72. $13^{2} =$ _______________

73. $17^{3} =$ _______________

74. $19^{-2} =$ _______________

75. $17^{-2} =$ _______________

76. $19^{3} =$ _______________

77. $7^{3} =$ _______________

78. $14^{-2} =$ _______________

79. $3^{-3} =$ _______________

80. $8^{-3} =$ _______________

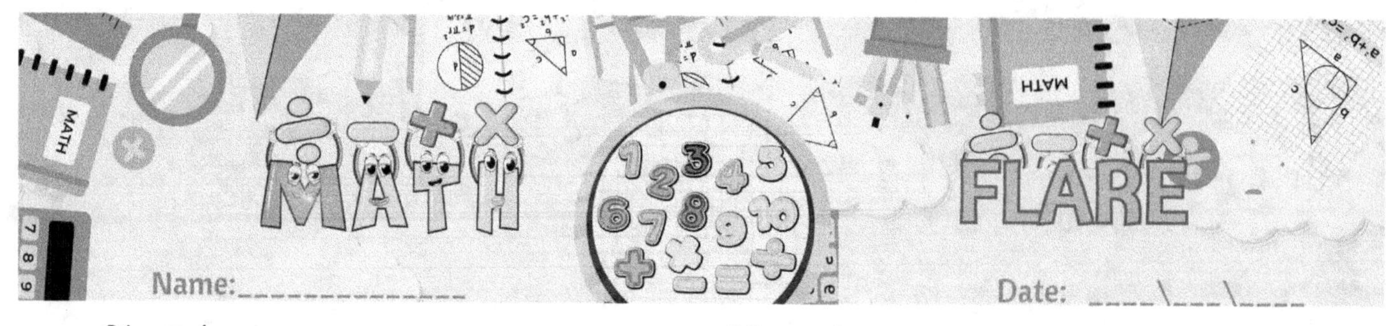

81. $3^4 =$ _______________

82. $11^2 =$ _______________

83. $3^{-2} =$ _______________

84. $14^4 =$ _______________

85. $15^2 =$ _______________

86. $7^2 =$ _______________

87. $20^{-2} =$ _______________

88. $20^2 =$ _______________

89. $1^2 =$ _______________

90. $3^3 =$ _______________

91. $2^{-3} =$ _______________

92. $10^{-3} =$ _______________

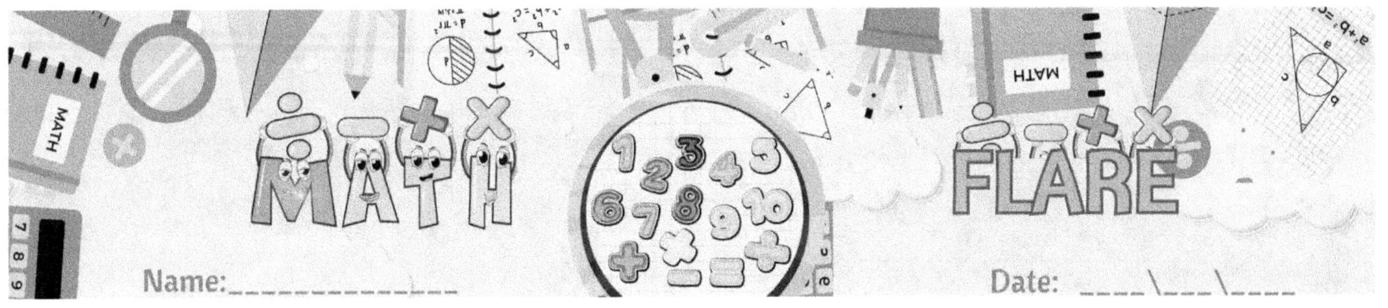

93. $1^{-2} =$ _______________

94. $6^{-2} =$ _______________

95. $9^{-2} =$ _______________

96. $20^{3} =$ _______________

97. $2^{3} =$ _______________

98. $20^{4} =$ _______________

99. $10^{2} =$ _______________

100. $4^{-2} =$ _______________

101. $2^{4} =$ _______________

102. $6^{4} =$ _______________

103. $17^{2} =$ _______________

104. $10^{-2} =$ _______________

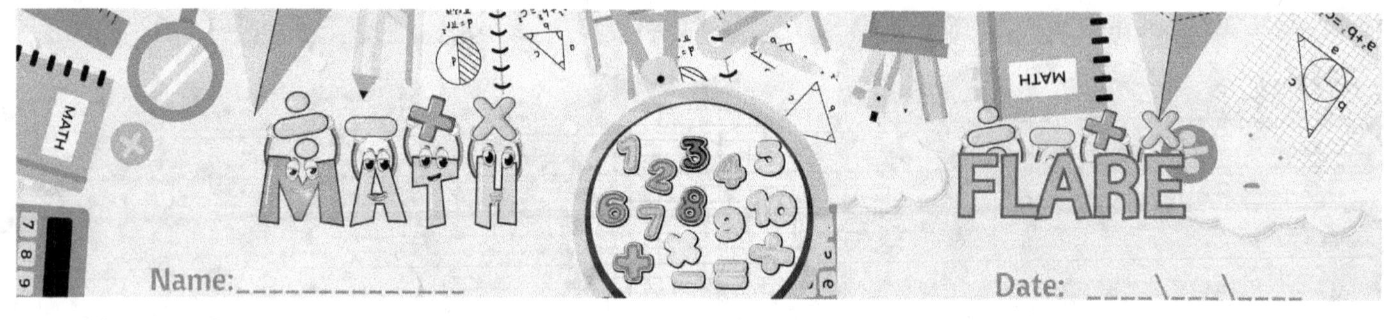

105. $14^3 =$ _______________

106. $15^4 =$ _______________

107. $5^4 =$ _______________

108. $11^{-2} =$ _______________

109. $19^2 =$ _______________

110. $19^{-3} =$ _______________

111. $18^4 =$ _______________

112. $12^{-2} =$ _______________

113. $11^3 =$ _______________

114. $14^{-3} =$ _______________

115. $12^4 =$ _______________

116. $7^{-2} =$ _______________

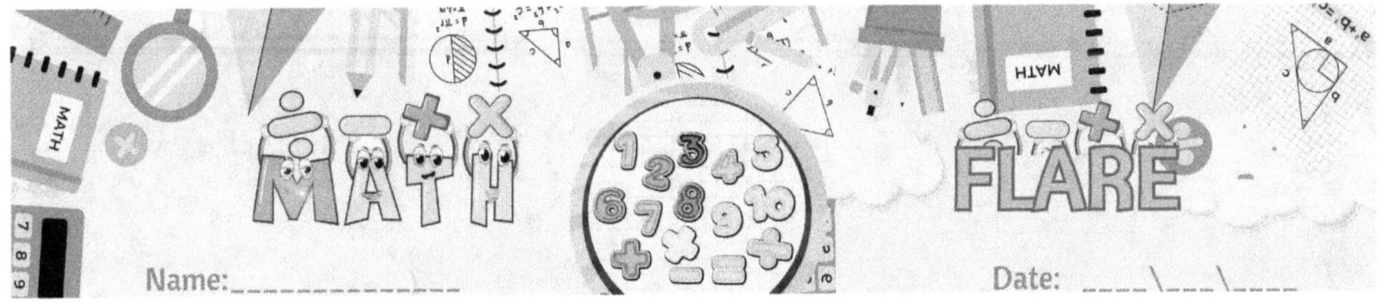

Square and Cube Roots

Calculate the root of each value.

117. $\sqrt[4]{256}$ = _______________

118. $\sqrt[4]{16}$ = _______________

119. $\sqrt[3]{8}$ = _______________

120. $\sqrt{25}$ = _______________

121. $\sqrt[4]{81}$ = _______________

122. $\sqrt{324}$ = _______________

123. $\sqrt[4]{2,401}$ = _______________

121. $\sqrt[3]{1,000}$ = _______________

125. $\sqrt[3]{216}$ = _______________

126. $\sqrt[3]{343}$ = _______________

127. $\sqrt[3]{64}$ = _______________

128. $\sqrt[4]{1,296}$ = _______________

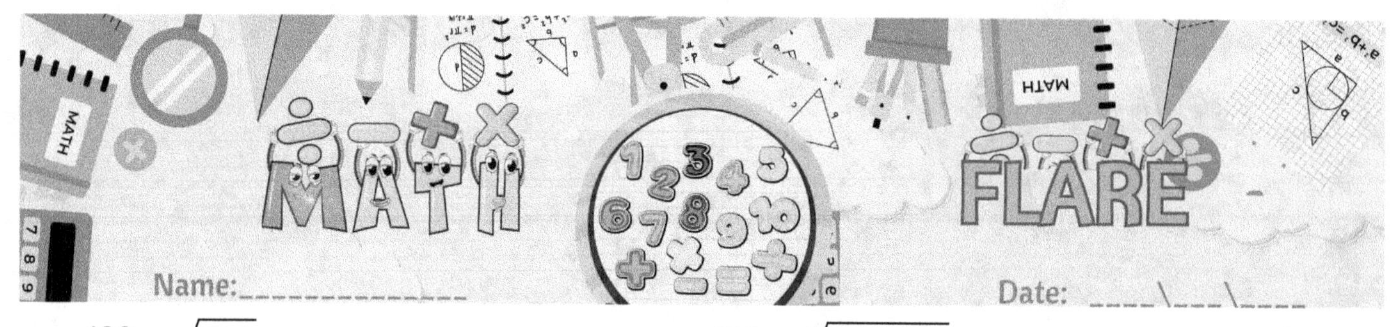

129. $\sqrt{36}$ = ________________

130. $\sqrt[3]{8,000}$ = ________________

131. $\sqrt{4}$ = ________________

132. $\sqrt{1}$ = ________________

133. $\sqrt[4]{1}$ = ________________

134. $\sqrt{9,409}$ = ________________

135. $\sqrt[4]{625}$ = ________________

136. $\sqrt{289}$ = ________________

137. $\sqrt[3]{9,261}$ = ________________

138. $\sqrt{676}$ = ________________

139. $\sqrt[3]{1}$ = ________________

140. $\sqrt{529}$ = ________________

141. $\sqrt[4]{10,000}$ = ________________

142. $\sqrt{9}$ = ________________

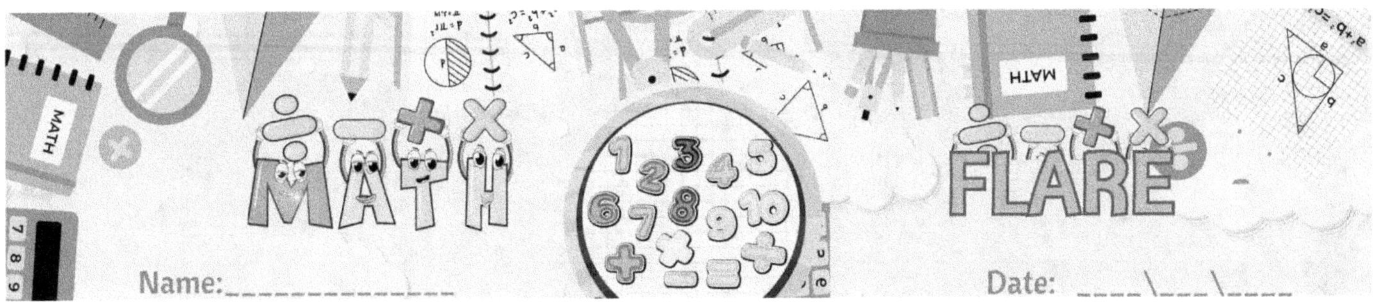

143. $\sqrt[3]{4,096}$ = _______________

144. $\sqrt[3]{5,832}$ = _______________

145. $\sqrt{81}$ = _______________

146. $\sqrt[3]{512}$ = _______________

147. $\sqrt[3]{27}$ = _______________

148. $\sqrt{7,396}$ = _______________

149. $\sqrt{784}$ = _______________

150. $\sqrt[3]{729}$ = _______________

151. $\sqrt{841}$ = _______________

152. $\sqrt{9,801}$ = _______________

153. $\sqrt[4]{4,096}$ = _______________

154. $\sqrt{8,649}$ = _______________

155. $\sqrt[3]{2,197}$ = _______________

156. $\sqrt[3]{125}$ = _______________

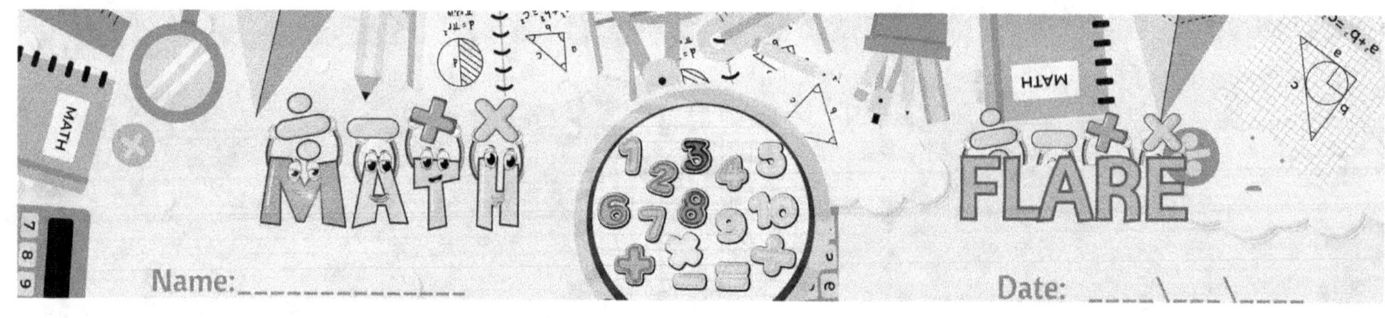

Order of Operations (PEMDAS)
Evaluate Expressions.

157. $10 + 1 + 3 =$

158. $(5^2) \times (4^2) + 3 =$

159. $3 + 6^2 + 6 + 7^2 =$

160. $9 + 7 - 8 + 1 =$

161. $9 + 4^2 + 6 + 10^2 =$

162. $9 \times 7 + 10 =$

163. $(5 + 7)^2 + (6 + 3)^2 =$

164. $(6 + 8) \div 8 =$

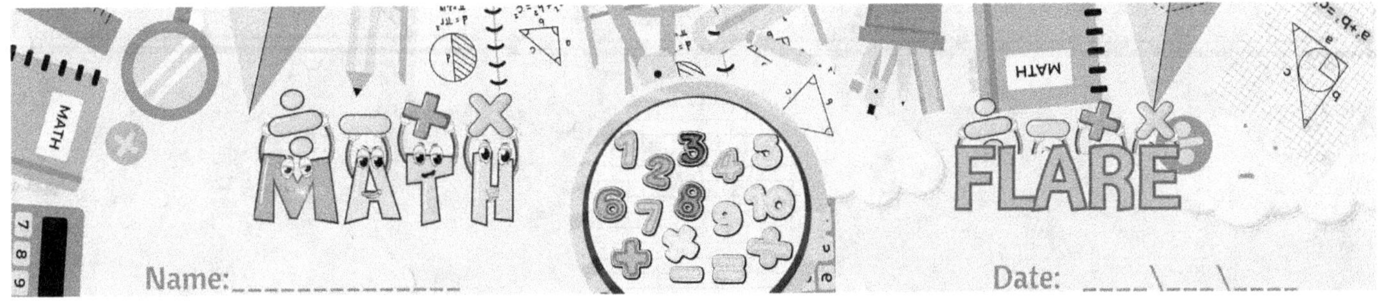

165. $(2 + 10) \times (6 + 3) =$

166. $(9 + 6) \times (3 + 6) =$

167. $(4 + 8) \times (6 + 2) =$

168. $5 + 9^2 =$

169. $1(6 + 7) =$

170. $3 \times 6 + 3 =$

171. $(7 + 1)^2 =$

172. $8 + 8^2 + 6 + 4^2 =$

173. $(8 + 6) \times (4 + 8) =$

174. $2 + 8^2 =$

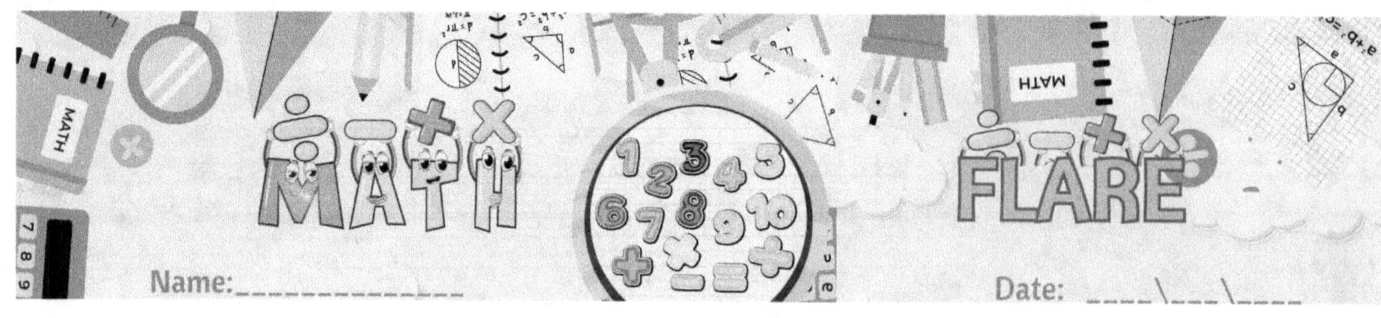

175. $(6 + 5) \times (4 + 7) =$

176. $2(7 + 9) =$

177. $3 + 9^2 + 3 + 10^2 =$

178. $9(4 + 7) =$

179. $(2^2) \times (1^2) + 4 =$

180. $(2 + 10)^2 =$

181. $(1 + 1)(5 + 2) =$

182. $(2 + 3) \times (8 + 8) =$

183. $(6 + 9) \div 7 =$

184. $3 \times 6 =$

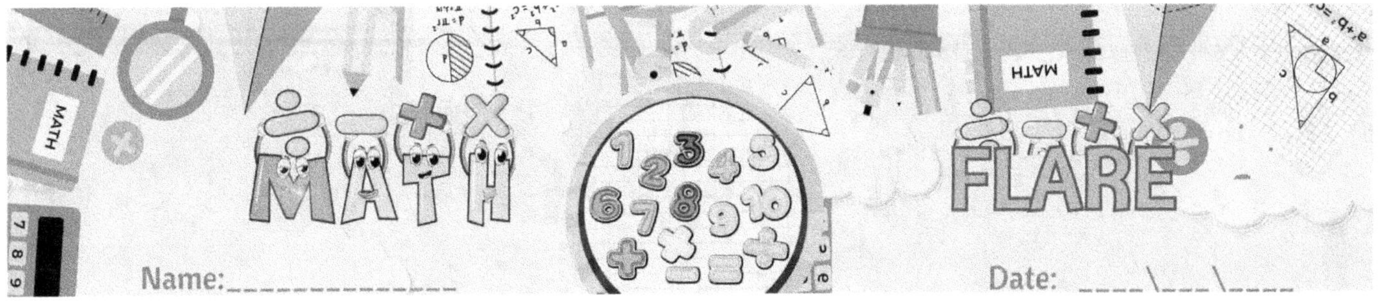

185. $6 \times 9 + 6 =$

186. $(1 + 6)(5 + 5) =$

187. $10(4 + 4) =$

188. $(5 + 5)^2 + (1 + 9)^2 =$

189. $(5 + 9)^2 =$

190. $2 \times (7 + 3) =$

191. $(3 + 8)^2 + (2 + 7)^2 =$

192. $2 \times 4 =$

193. $(2 + 5) \div 4 =$

194. $(9^2) \times (4^2) + 5 =$

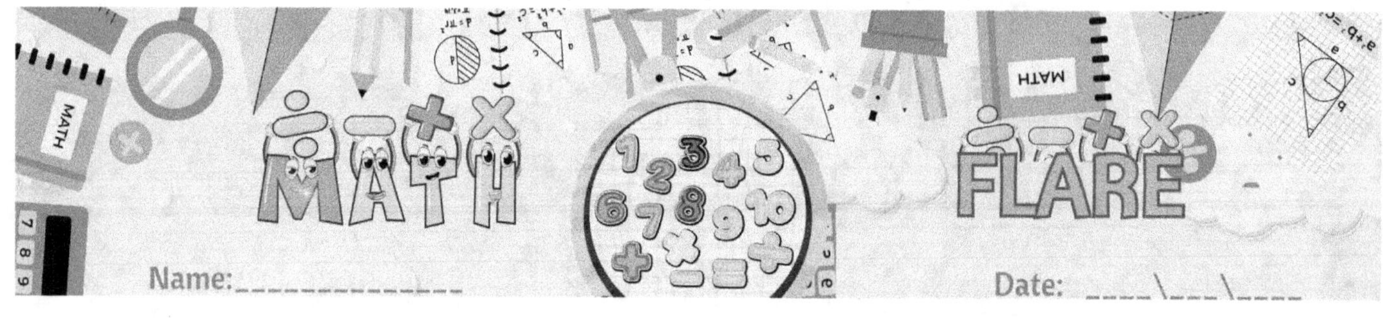

Name:________________   Date: _____ \ ___ \ _____

195. $2 + 10^2 + 5 + 3^2 =$

196. $5 + 1 - 2 + 6 =$

197. $9(7 + 10) =$

198. $7 \times (8 + 10) =$

199. $7 \times 2 \times 4 =$

200. $4 + 9 + 4 + 2 =$

201. $5 + 1^2 + 8 + 5^2 =$

202. $3 + 5 + 7 =$

203. $(4 + 10)^2 + (2 + 2)^2 =$

204. $1 + 10 + 3 =$

205. $(6 \times 7) - (7 + 10) =$

206. $8 \times 10 =$

207. $2 + 4 + 6 + 9 =$

208. $(5 + 10)^2 + (2 + 8)^2 =$

209. $1 \times 2 =$

210. $10 \times (10 + 10) =$

211. $(3^2) \times (8^2) + 9 =$

212. $7 + 9 + 3 =$

213. $7(6 + 3) =$

214. $9 + 6 + 9 =$

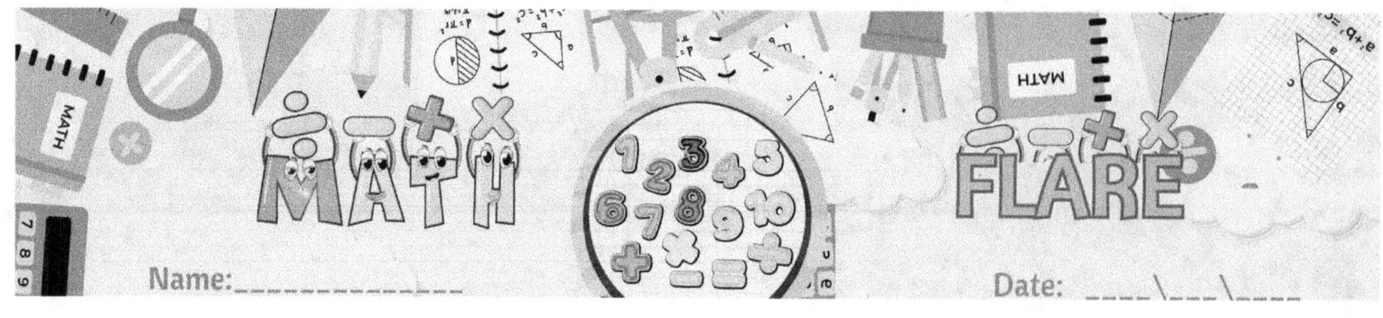

215. $7 \times (9 + 8) =$

216. $(2 + 6) \times (8 + 4) =$

217. $(2^2) \times (4^2) + 10 =$

218. $2 + 6 - 10 + 10 =$

219. $4 + 4 + 10 =$

220. $(4 + 9) \div 2 =$

221. $(2 + 1) \times (7 + 6) =$

222. $(8 + 7)^2 =$

223. $(2 + 5)(10 + 5) =$

224. $1 + 1^2 + 9 + 1^2 =$

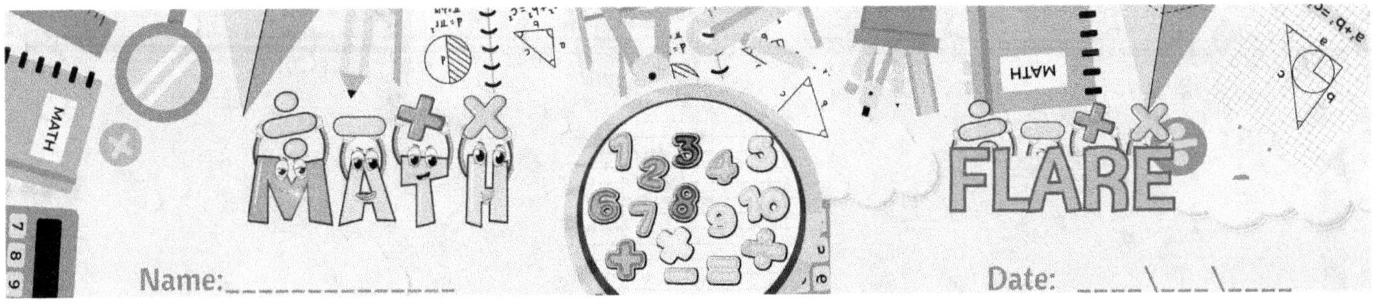

225. $5 \times 6 =$

226. $5 + 5 + 6 + 9 =$

227. $6 \times 4 + 6 =$

228. $4 \times 7 =$

229. $(10 + 10)(3 + 6) =$

230. $9 + 1 + 4 =$

231. $8 + 6 + 3 =$

232. $(2 + 6) \div 6 =$

233. $10 \times 8 + 1 =$

234. $(9^2) \times (1^2) + 7 =$

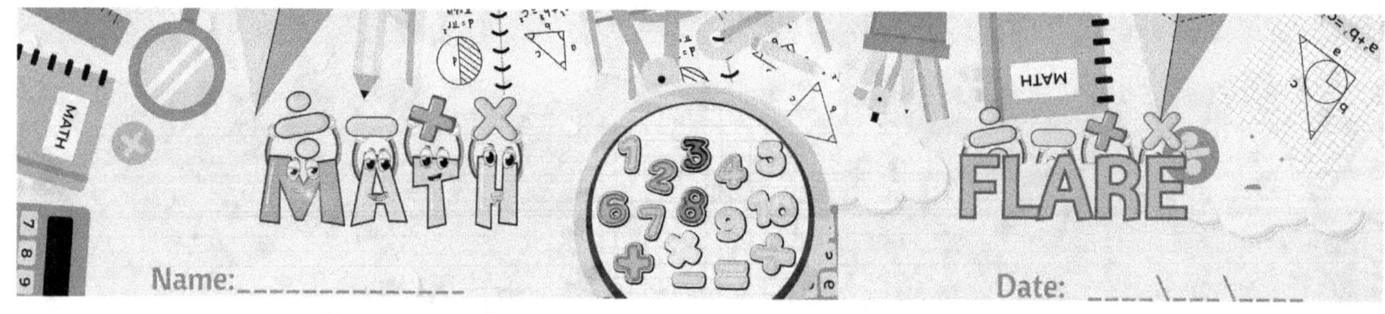

235. $6(9 + 1) =$

236. $3 \times 10 \times 4 =$

237. $(9 + 5)^2 =$

238. $(7 + 3) \times (5 + 3) =$

239. $10 + 3 + 4 =$

240. $(8 + 8)^2 + (9 + 10)^2 =$

241. $(1^2) \times (5^2) + 7 =$

242. $4 \times 4 + 9 =$

243. $3 + 1 - 10 + 5 =$

244. $9 \times (9 + 8) =$

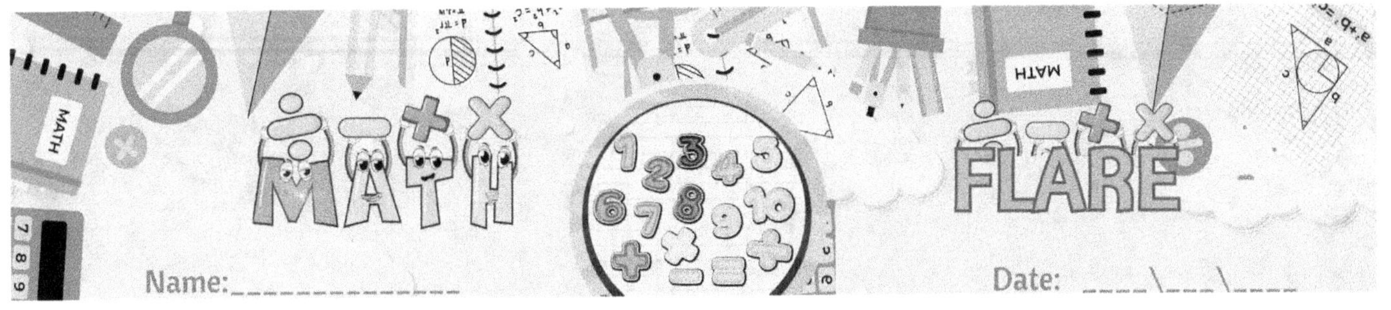

245. $(3 \times 10) - (9 + 8) =$

246. $9 + 8^2 =$

247. $4 + 2^2 =$

248. $(1 + 6) \div 8 =$

249. $(5 + 1)^2 =$

250. $10 \times (2 + 3) =$

251. $(3 + 2) \times (10 + 2) =$

252. $10 \times 1 \times 3 =$

253. $9 + 6 + 8 =$

254. $(5 + 7) \times (4 + 10) =$

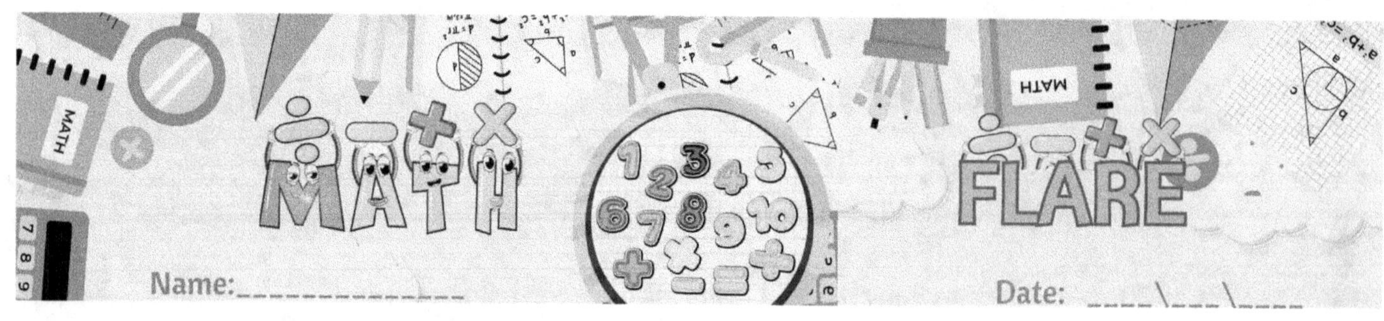

Equations (One Side)
Solve for the variable.

255. $4 + x = 20$

256. $5 + 10m = 25$

257. $12 \times y = 228$

258. $m + 13 = 17$

259. $150 \div y = 15$

260. $13 - m = 8$

261. $x \times 7 = 77$

262. $y \times 5 = 100$

263. $72 - 10y = 2$

264. $4z + 3 = 39$

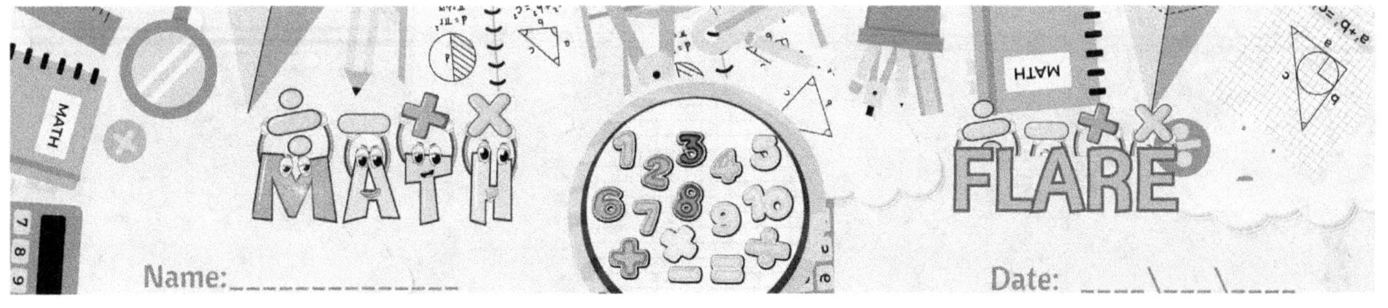

265. $k \times 20 = 200$

266. $150 \div m = 10$

267. $18x + 6 = 222$

268. $5y + 12 = 52$

269. $13 - 5z = 3$

270. $10m + 14 = 194$

271. $12 \times k = 168$

272. $m \times 20 = 280$

273. $9m - 9 = 126$

274. $k - 6 = 10$

275. $3 + 9z = 120$

276. $7 + m = 8$

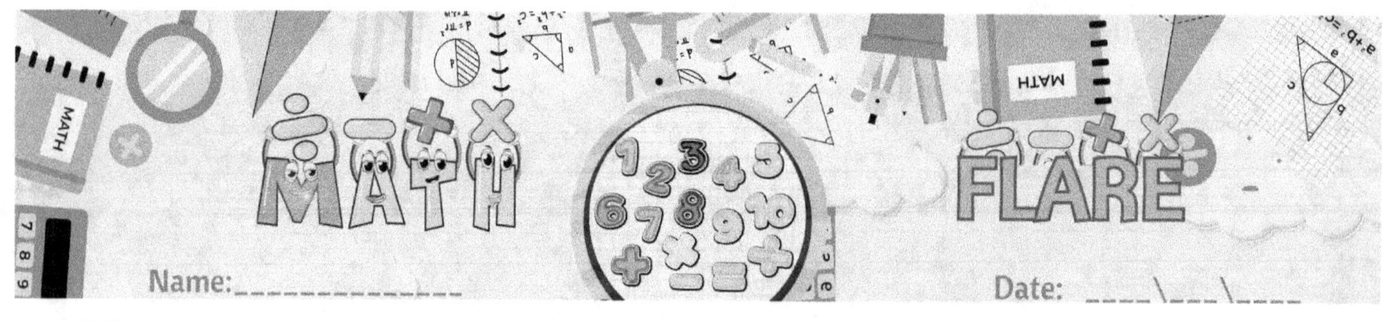

277. $332 - 19z = 9$

278. $x + 5 = 17$

279. $1 + y = 8$

280. $131 - 13y = 1$

281. $3z + 18 = 24$

282. $149 - 18z = 5$

283. $z \times 3 = 45$

284. $m + 9 = 18$

285. $10 + 6z = 70$

286. $k + 15 = 28$

287. $k - 7 = 13$

288. $x \times 14 = 42$

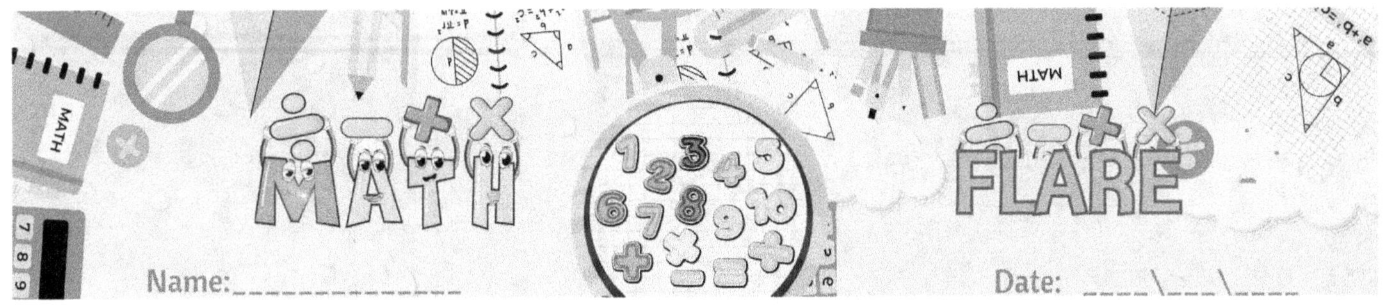

289. $20 + 3y = 71$

290. $144 \div m = 18$

291. $249 - 20x = 9$

292. $2 \times x = 28$

293. $7z + 4 = 11$

294. $4 + k = 14$

295. $66 \div z = 11$

296. $11 + 15z = 146$

297. $m + 15 = 32$

298. $6 + 15m = 291$

299. $k + 15 = 27$

300. $14 + y = 16$

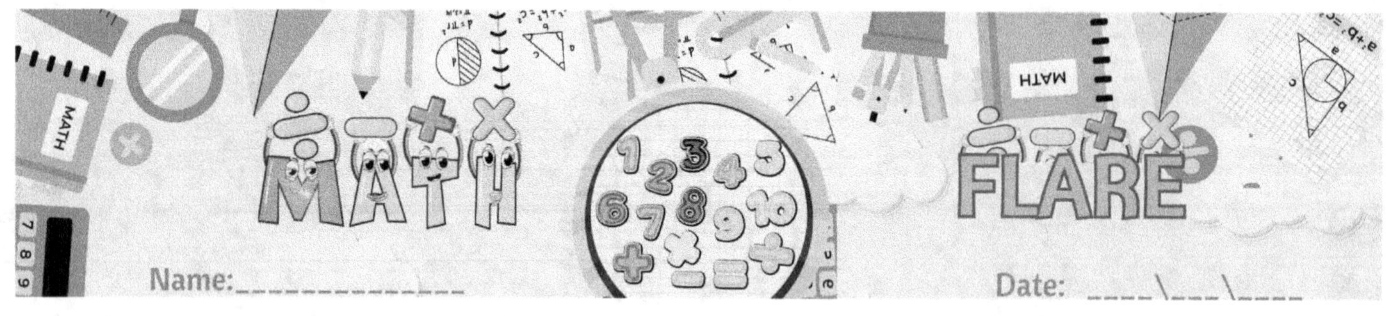

301. $y \div 14 = 6$

302. $10m + 16 = 206$

303. $x \times 18 = 324$

304. $4m + 11 = 23$

305. $15x + 18 = 303$

306. $12 \div k = 12$

307. $z \div 7 = 4$

308. $13z + 6 = 201$

309. $10 \times y = 120$

310. $4 \div m = 2$

311. $198 - 15x = 3$

312. $5 \times m = 15$

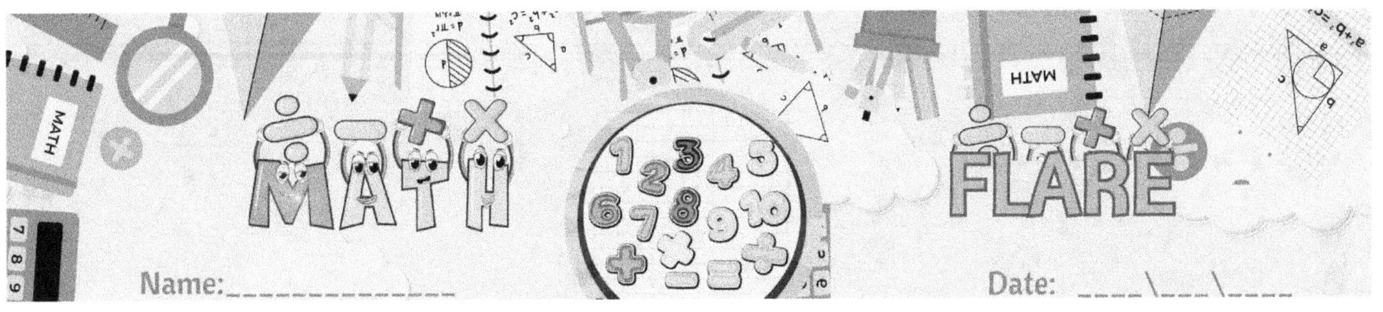

Equations (Two Sides)
Solve for the variable.

313. $1 + 5z + 2 = 46 + z + -7$

314. $9 + 8k = 72 - k$

315. $9y + 1 = 16 - 6y$

316. $5k = 32 + k$

317. $24 + m = 7m$

318. $7 + 6x = 14 - x$

319. $15 - y = 6 + 4y + 4$

320. $19 + z = 8 + 2z + 4$

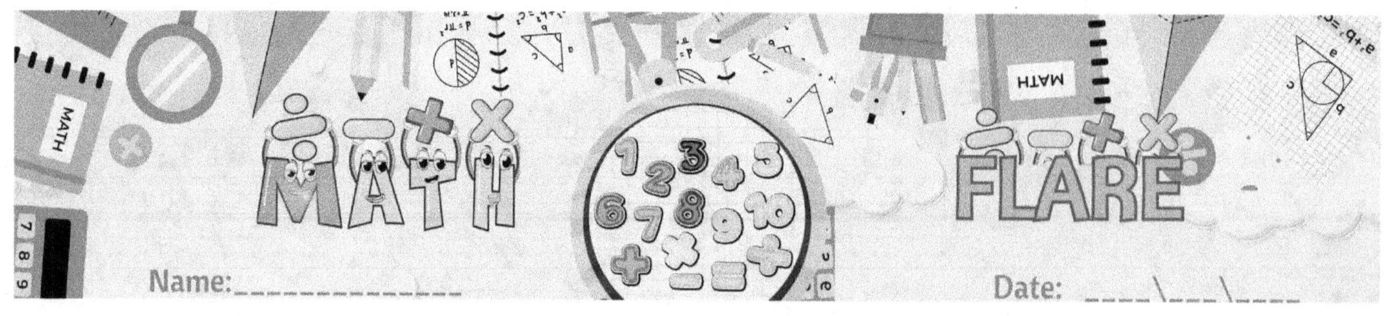

321. $28 - z + 15 = 7 + 3z + 4$

322. $1 + 5m = 3 + 4m$

323. $5y = 30 - y$

324. $2 + 2z + 9 = 16 + z$

325. $87 - 6z = 3 + 8z$

326. $5 + 8z = 15 - 2z$

327. $2z = 18 - z$

328. $9 + 6m + 4 = 55 - m$

329. $16 + m = 3m + 2$

330. $5 + 5z = 17 + z$

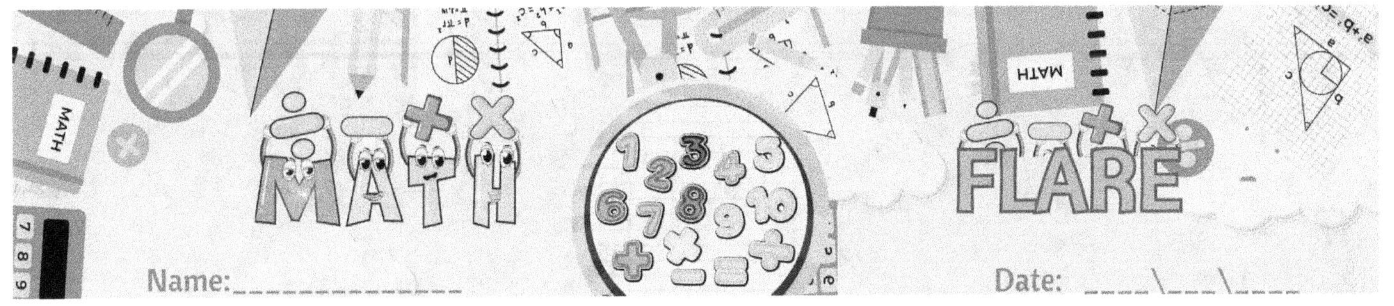

331. $45 + 3x = 9x + 3$

332. $7 + 3k + 9 = 28 + k$

333. $73 - y + 15 = 7 + 8y + 9$

334. $15 + y + 0 = 2 + 6y + 3$

335. $7m = 48 + m$

336. $8 + 9y = 25 - 8y$

337. $19 + y = 5 + 2y + 6$

338. $9 + m = 2m$

339. $3 + 4y + 6 = 15 + y$

340. $15 + m = 4 + 2m + 3$

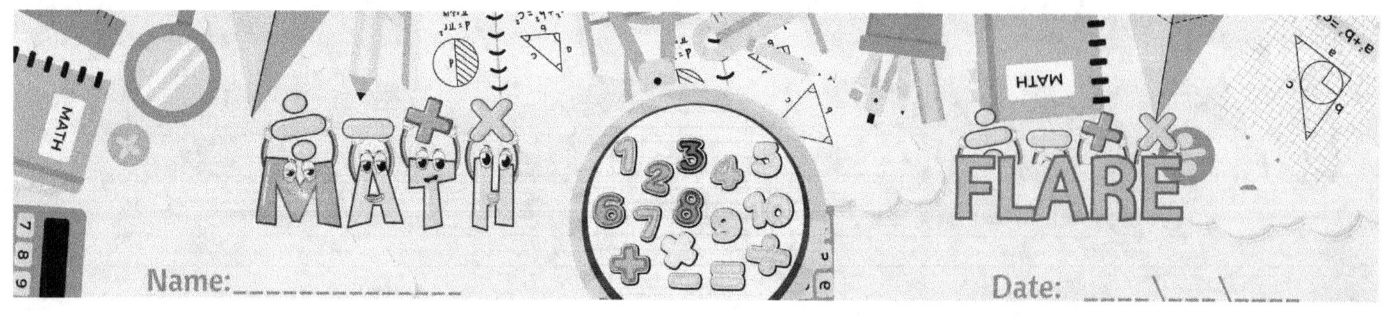

341. $42 + k + -7 = 1 + 5k + 2$

342. $8m + 3 = 9 + 6m$

343. $19 + k = 4k + 4$

344. $23 - 2y = 3y + 8$

345. $6 + 8z + 9 = 69 - z$

346. $4y + 5 = 32 + y$

347. $1 + 8x = 66 - 5x$

348. $4 + 3y = 6 + y$

349. $23 + m = 8m + 2$

350. $20 - y + 16 = 6 + 2y + 9$

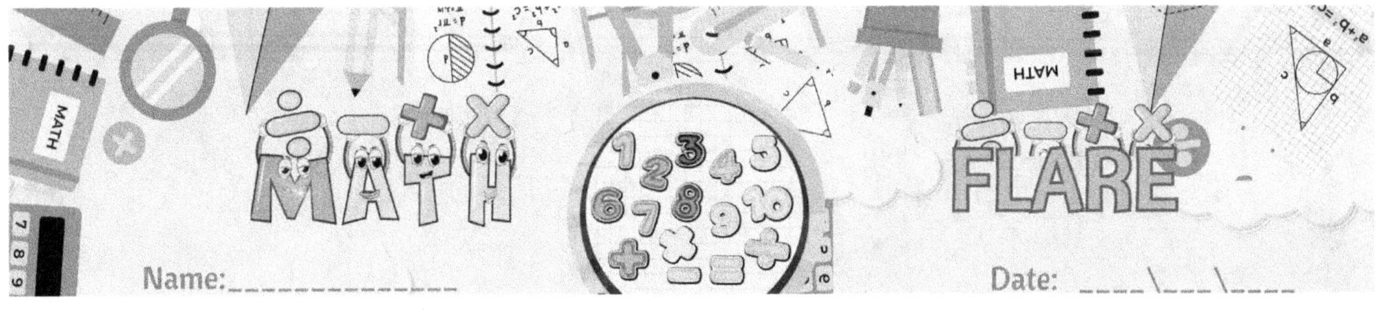

351. $9 + 8y = 13 + 7y$

352. $18 + y = 7y$

353. $7m + 6 = 51 - 2m$

354. $29 - y = 5 + 5y$

355. $1 + 6z = 22 - z$

356. $10 + k = 3k + 2$

357. $5 + 7k + 4 = 45 + k$

358. $4 + 2k + 6 = 24 - k + 13$

359. $39 + k = 5 + 7k + 4$

360. $2 + 9x = 146 - 7x$

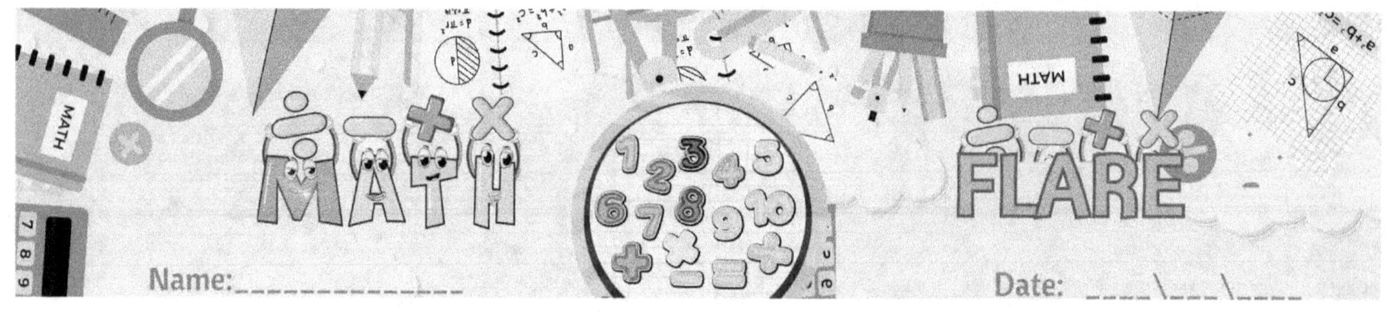

361. $57 + k + 1 = 1 + 8k + 8$

362. $9 + 9z = 43 - 8z$

363. $70 - x = 8x + 7$

364. $18 - m = 2 + 2m + 7$

365. $11 + z = 5 + 4z$

366. $17 - k = 3k + 1$

367. $1 + 3x = 33 - x$

368. $16 - k = 7k$

369. $45 - y = 3y + 9$

370. $20 - k = 3k$

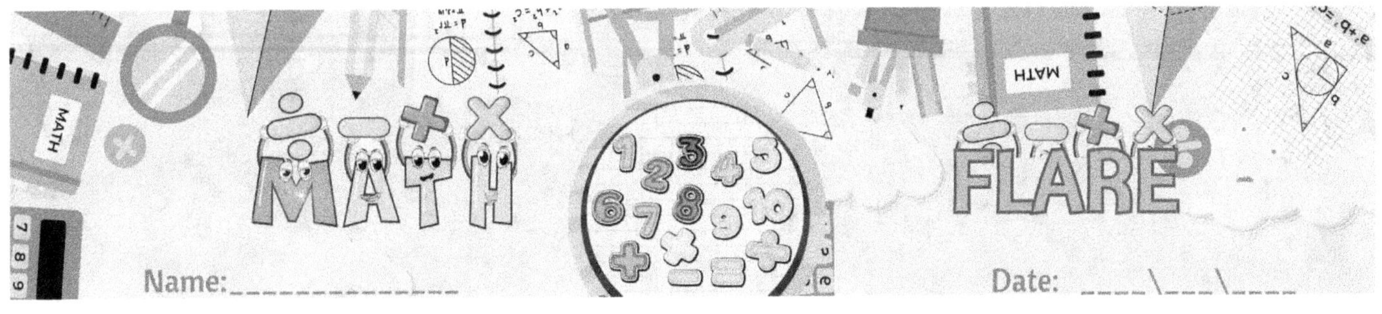

Solving Inequalities

371.
$$-5 > -3y$$

372.
$$y + -7 \geq -10$$

373.
$$3 < \frac{z}{3}$$

374.
$$m - -8 \leq 8$$

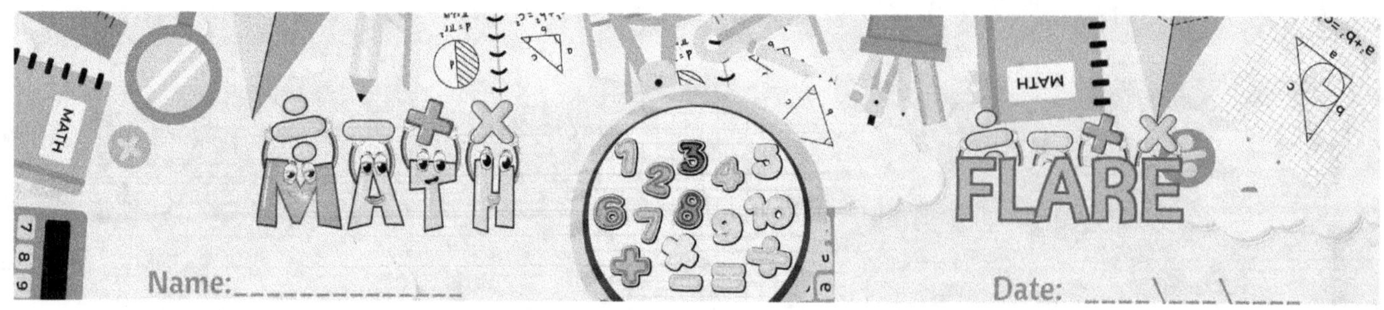

375.

$$9 + y < 4$$

376.

$$4 < m - 3$$

377.

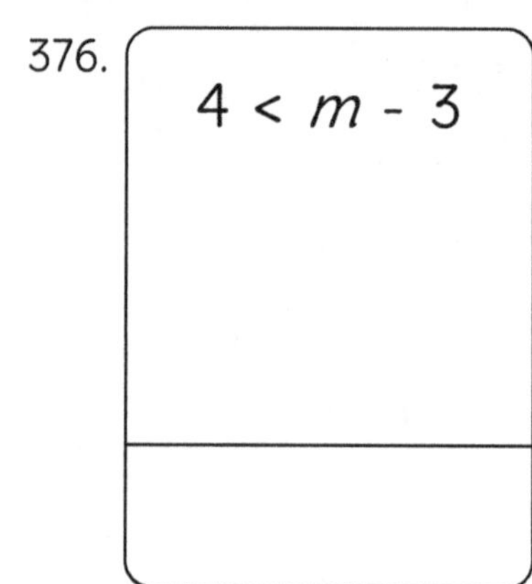

$$\frac{x}{-3} \geq 4$$

378.

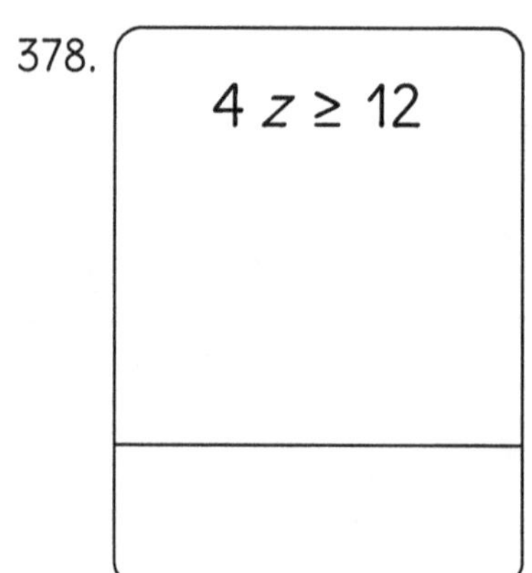

$$4z \geq 12$$

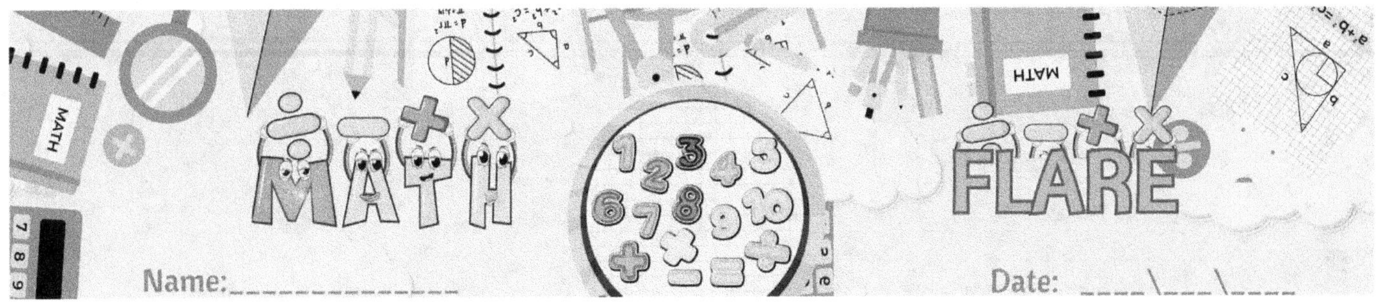

379.

$$4\,m < 6$$

380.

$$4 < \dfrac{k}{6}$$

381.

$$8 < -1 - x$$

382.

$$4 + z < -3$$

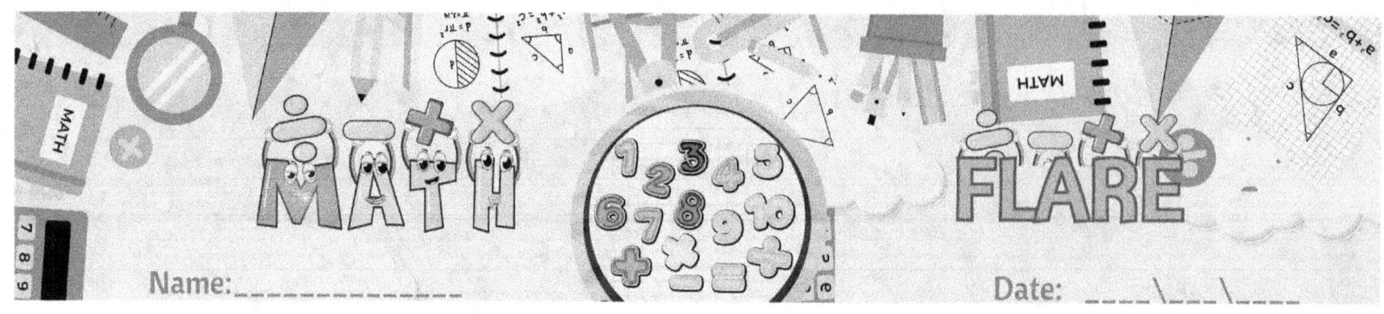

383.

$$-5k > -6$$

384.

$$7 \le y - -1$$

385.

$$8 < \frac{m}{-7}$$

386.

$$2 + y \le -4$$

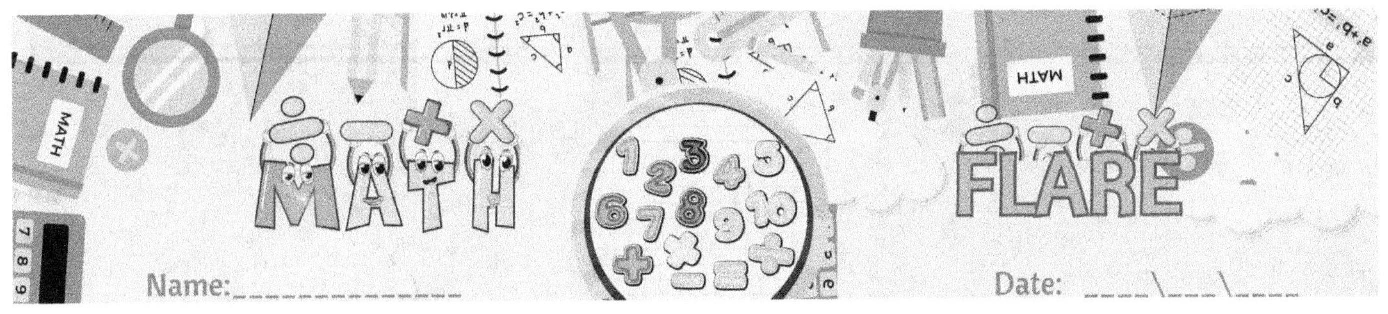

387.

$$\frac{y}{6} > 5$$

388.

$$12 \geq -6z$$

389.

$$3 + m \leq 8$$

390.

$$5 \geq 4 - z$$

391. 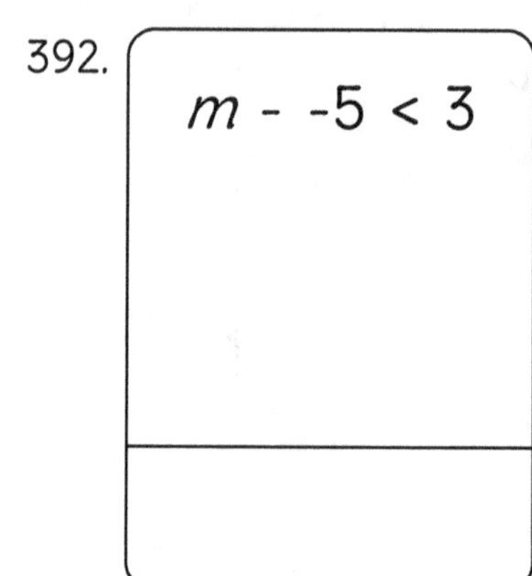

$$8 < \frac{x}{5}$$

392.

$$m - {-5} < 3$$

393.

$$-4 + x \geq 7$$

394.

$$-4z > -5$$

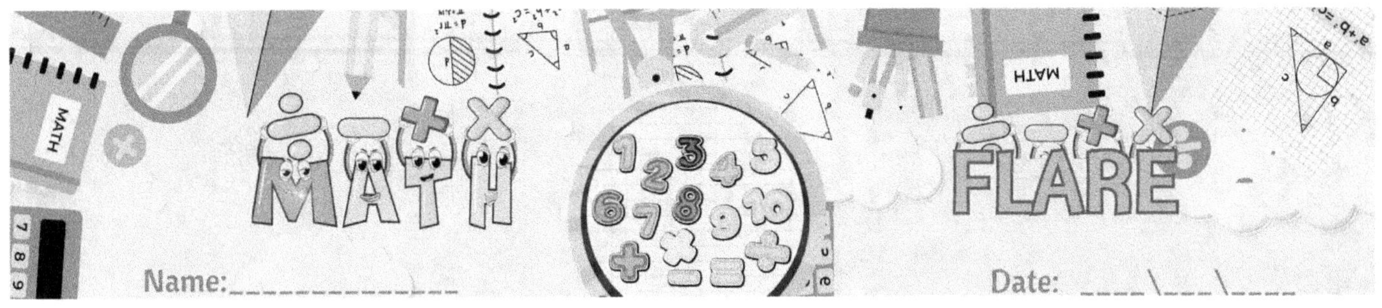

395.

$$-6 > -10z$$

396.

$$7 < x - -7$$

397.

$$4 < 3 + x$$

398.

$$3 > \frac{k}{8}$$

Name:______________ Date: ___________

399. $8 < m + 2$

400. $6 \leq -4y$

401. $-7 - k > -6$

402. $\frac{k}{-5} \geq 3$

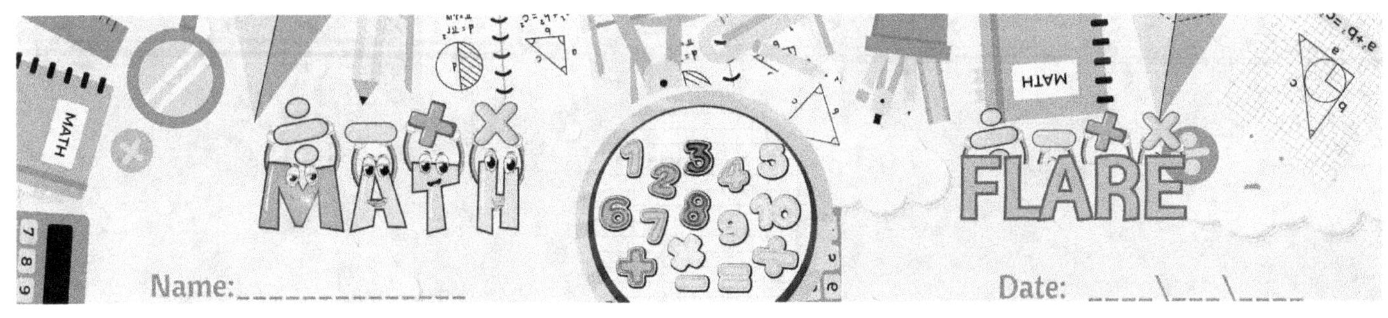

403.

$$\frac{m}{4} > 2$$

404.

$$15 > 9\,m$$

405.

$$-8 < y + {-2}$$

406.

$$k - 5 > 9$$

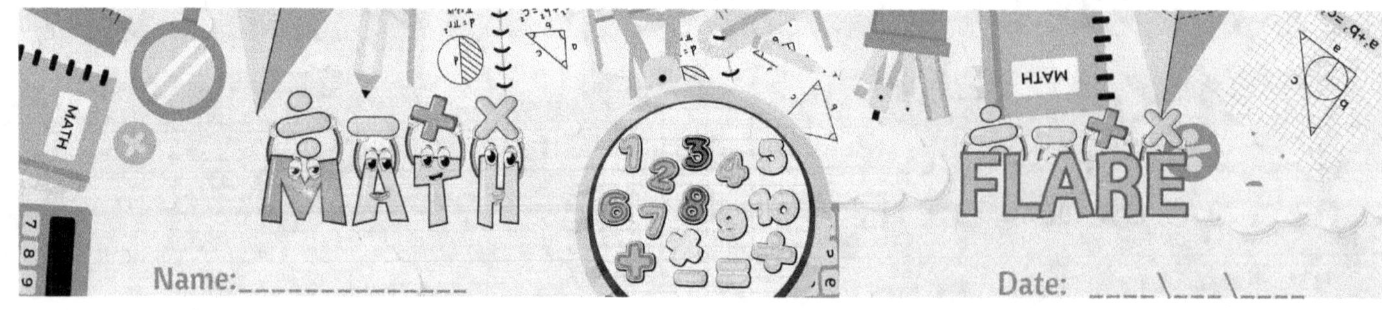

407.

$$x + \text{-}4 \leq \text{-}3$$

408.

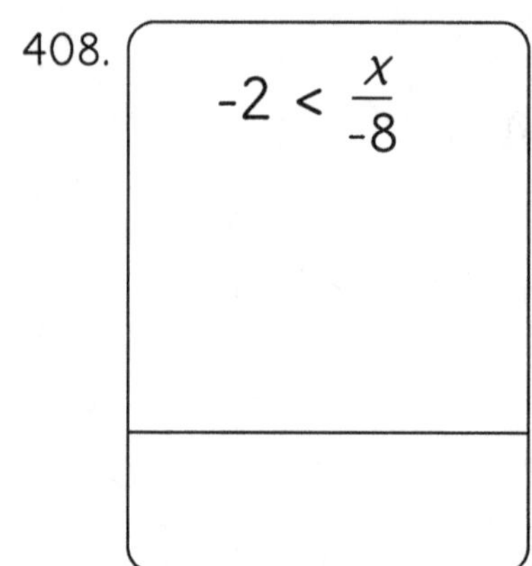
$$\text{-}2 < \frac{x}{\text{-}8}$$

409.

$$15 < 9\,k$$

410.

$$0 \leq x - \text{-}8$$

411.

$$9 < 8 - y$$

412.

$$12 \leq 2z$$

413.

$$-5 + m \geq 2$$

414.

$$-5 > \frac{x}{-2}$$

415.
$$-9\,m \le 15$$

416.
$$-6 + x < 2$$

417.
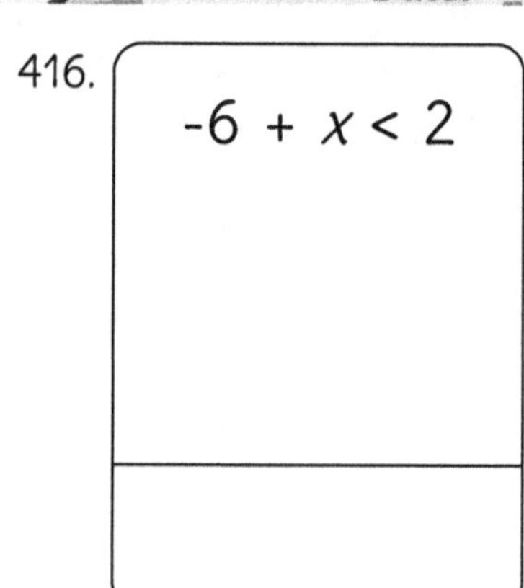
$$-1 < \frac{y}{-1}$$

418.
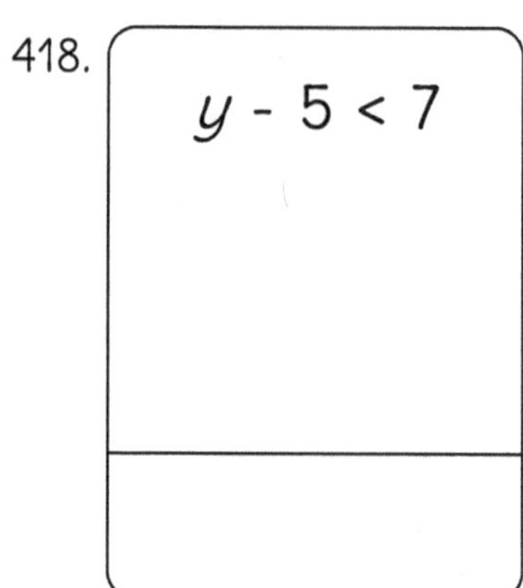
$$y - 5 < 7$$

419.

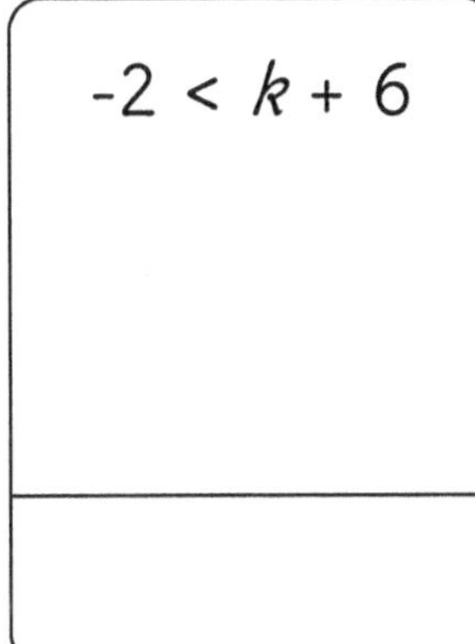

$$-2 < k + 6$$

420.

$$-4 > -9 - m$$

421.

$$-6 > \dfrac{z}{-8}$$

422.

$$12 > -18z$$

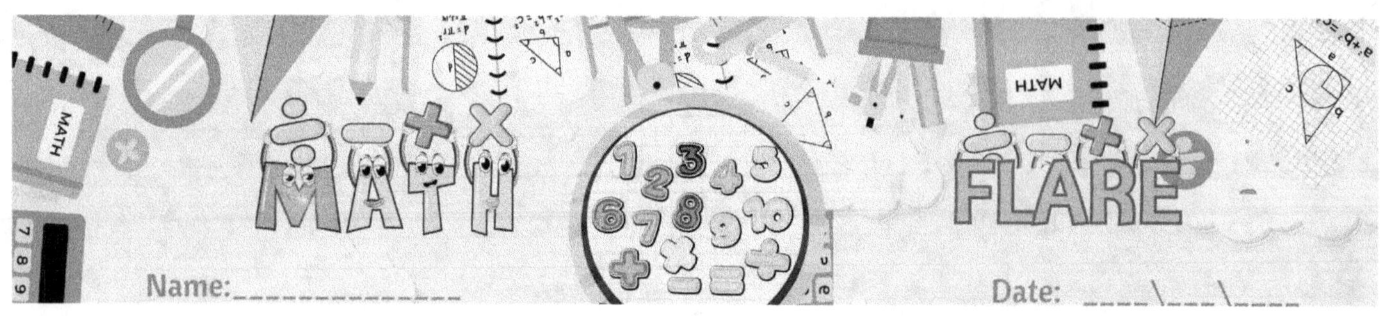

423.

$$-1 - m < 7$$

424.

$$\frac{k}{-5} > -6$$

425.

$$-12 < 2y$$

426.

$$-1 + x > 2$$

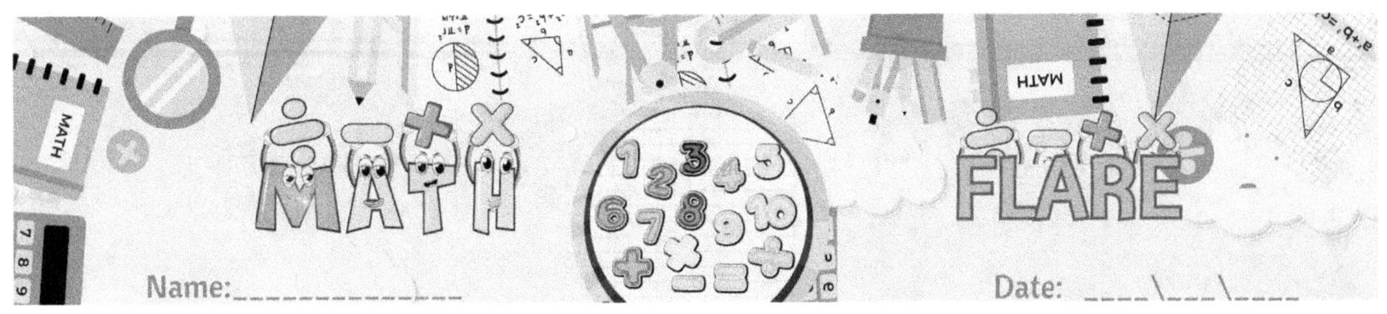

427.

$$8\,k \geq 4$$

428.

$$7 < 5 - k$$

429.

$$9 + x \leq 4$$

430.

$$-5 \geq \frac{m}{-9}$$

Name:_________________ Date: ____________

Solving Equations

Evaluate each expression when: x = 2

431. $3 + x =$

432. $x - 9 =$

433. $7 + x =$

434. $6 + x =$

435. $x + 10 =$

436. $x - 10 =$

437. $5 + x =$

438. $3 - x =$

439. $8 - x =$

440. $x - 8 =$

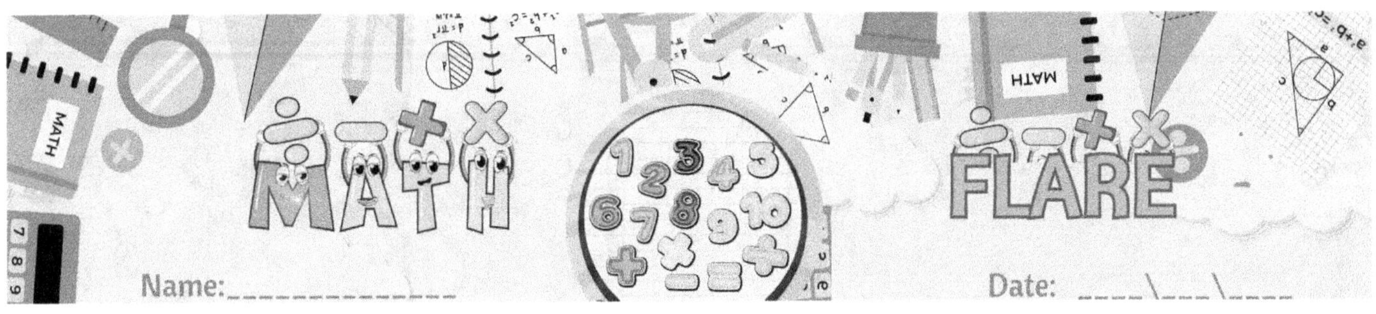

Solving Equations

Evaluate each expression when: x = 1

441. $x + 9 =$

442. $x + 10 =$

443. $4 - x =$

444. $x + 4 =$

445. $8 - x =$

446. $x - 6 =$

447. $1 + x =$

448. $x + 8 =$

449. $1 - x =$

450. $x - 7 =$

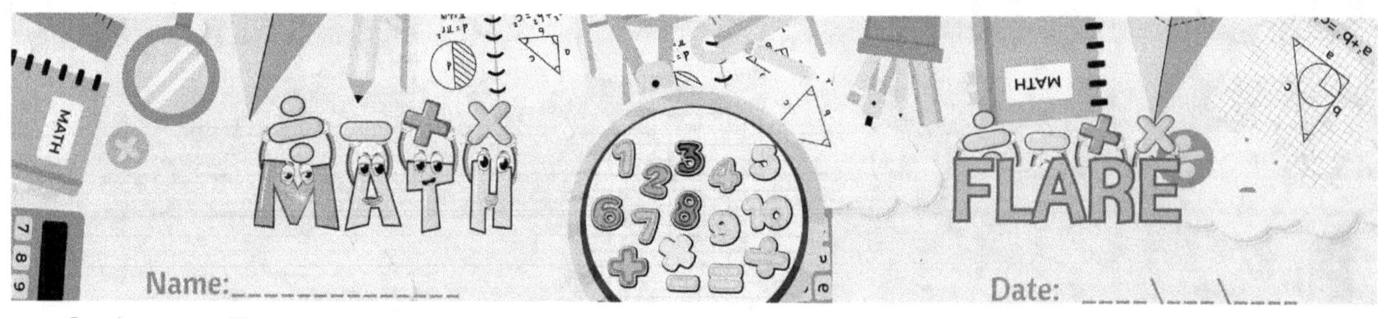

Solving Equations

Evaluate each expression when: x = 2

451. $x + 6 =$

452. $8 + x =$

453. $10 - x =$

454. $x + 4 =$

455. $3 + x =$

456. $x + 3 =$

457. $9 + x =$

458. $x + 5 =$

459. $10 + x =$

460. $8 - x =$

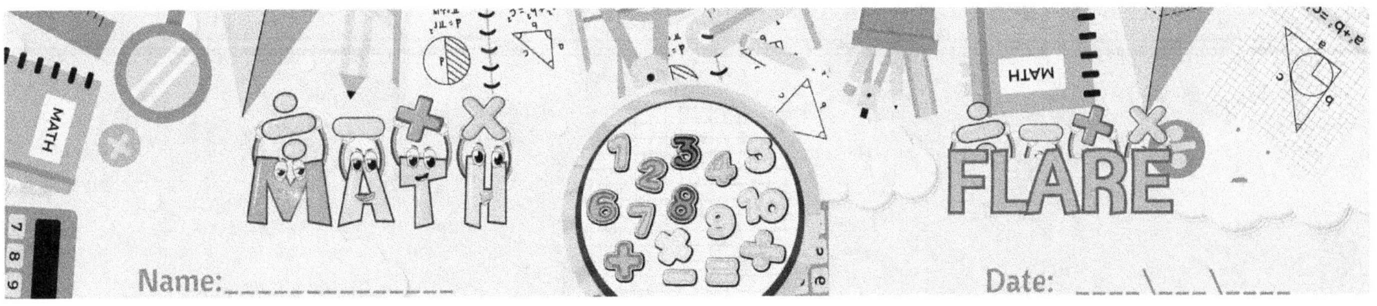

Solving Equations

Evaluate each expression when: x = 1

461. $9x + 4 =$

462. $x + 5 + 6x =$

463. $5 + 8x =$

464. $10x + 9 =$

465. $8 \div (x + 6) =$

466. $3x + 9 =$

467. $2x - x =$

468. $8x + 7 =$

469. $(7x)^1 =$

470. $5x + x =$

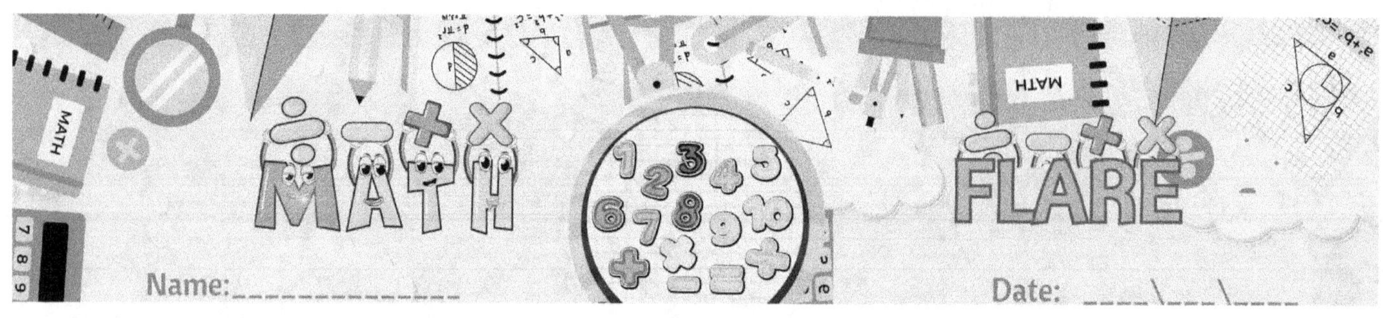

Solving Equations

Evaluate each expression when: $x = 2$

471. $5(7x) =$

472. $x^1 + x - 1 =$

473. $10x + x =$

474. $7x + 6 =$

475. $\dfrac{48}{x} =$

476. $x - 4 =$

477. $9x + 6 =$

478. $2(1 + x) =$

479. $x \div 1 =$

480. $x - 10 =$

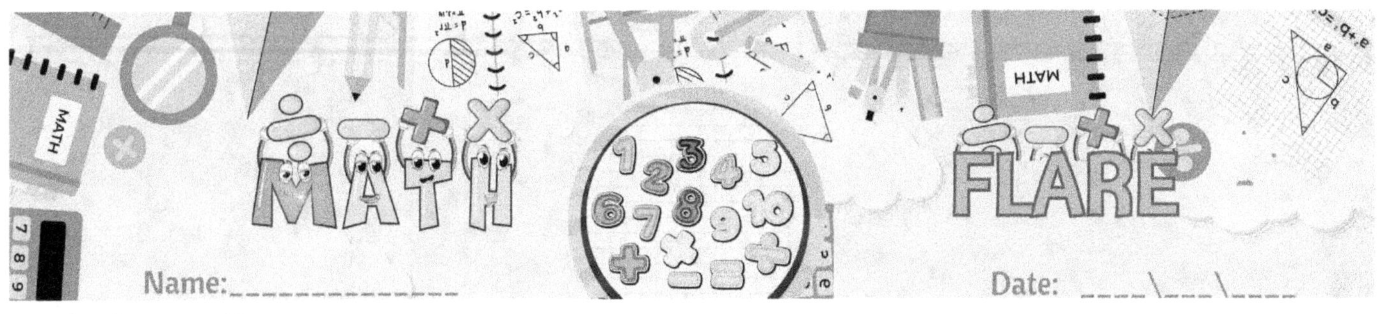

Solving Equations

Evaluate each expression when: x = 1

481. $x^1 + x - 3 =$

482. $7(x) =$

483. $\dfrac{x}{1} =$

484. $x - 6 =$

485. $1 + (7x + 4) =$

486. $(4x)^1 =$

487. $1 + 4x =$

488. $2 \div x + 5 =$

489. $3x + 4x + 6x =$

490. $5 + x =$

Solving Equations

Evaluate each expression when: x = 1

491. $(x^1 + 9) - 5(2 + x) =$

492. $x + x =$

493. $1(1 + x) =$

494. $(10x + 5) + (10x - 4) =$

495. $(5x)(5x) =$

496. $6x + 8 =$

497. $10 + x =$

498. $1 \div x =$

499. $7 - x =$

500. $3 - x =$

Solving Equations

Evaluate each expression when: $x = 2$

501. $x - 7 =$

502. $x - 1 =$

503. $10(6x) =$

504. $6 - x =$

505. $(9x + 9) + (3x - 1) =$

506. $(5 + 4x) + (9x - 6) - (1 + 3x) =$

507. $7x + 8 - 10x =$

508. $x^1 + x - 5 =$

509. $(x^1 + 10) - 4(2 + x) =$

510. $7x + 10 + (4x - 8) =$

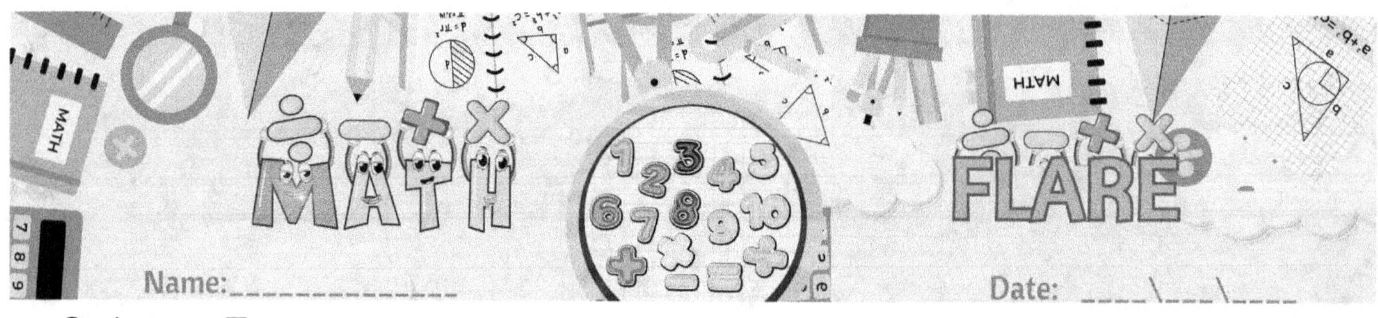

Solving Equations

Evaluate each expression when: $x = 4$

511. $10x - x =$

512. $3x + 1 =$

513. $3 + \dfrac{32}{x} + 4^1 =$

514. $2^1 + x^1 =$

515. $5(9x - 9) + 6(3 + x) =$

516. $x + 1 + 7x =$

517. $7x + 5 =$

518. $2(3 - x) =$

519. $x^1 + x - 3 =$

520. $3 \div (x + 9) =$

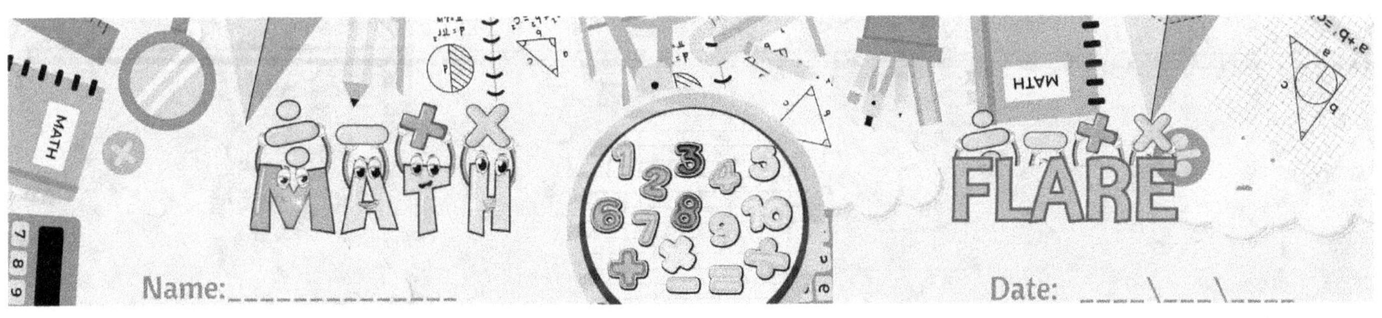

Solving Equations

Evaluate each expression when: $x = 5$

521. $\dfrac{8 + x}{x + 8} =$

522. $5x - 10 + 9x =$

523. $x(4 + x) =$

524. $10x + 5 =$

525. $4x + 10x - 8 =$

526. $5 + 9x =$

527. $7x + 6x + 10x =$

528. $8x - x =$

529. $6(6 - x) =$

530. $\dfrac{50}{x} =$

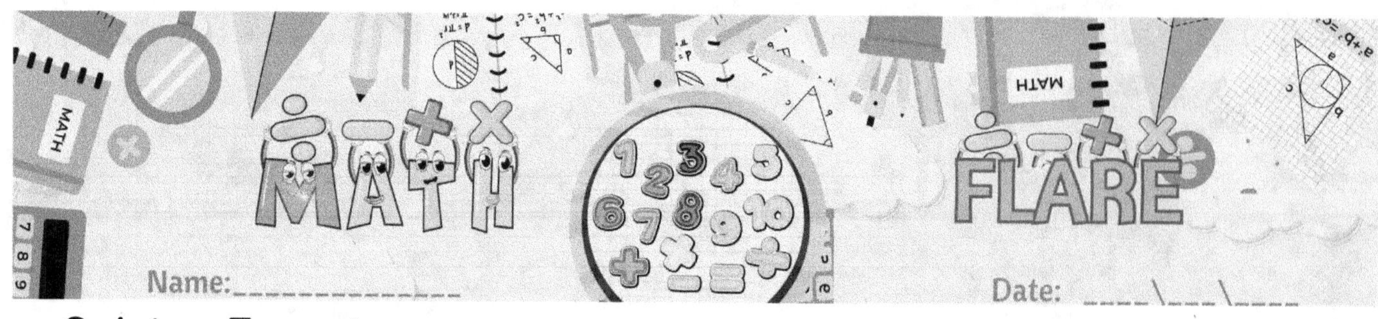

Solving Equations

Evaluate each expression when: $x = 2$

531. $3(6 + x) =$

532. $2(7 - x) =$

533. $5(10 - x) =$

534. $(2x)(2x) =$

535. $5x + 8 =$

536. $x^1 + x - 7 =$

537. $7(9 + x) =$

538. $6x + x =$

539. $7 + \dfrac{x}{2} =$

540. $x + 10 =$

ANSWERS

Page 1: Operations with Whole Numbers

1. -20	2. -3.5	3. -5	4. 810	5. 0.6	6. -210
7. -17	8. -4.5	9. 7	10. -11	11. 6	12. 14
13. 16	14. -2	15. 84	16. 20	17. -2	18. -1
19. -15	20. 126	21. -0.4	22. 0.4	23. 16	24. -10
25. 14	26. 56	27. -120	28. 45	29. -1	30. -8
31. 54	32. -2	33. 8	34. -26	35. -10	36. -13
37. 5	38. -567	39. 28	40. -10	41. 6	42. 8
43. -7	44. 8	45. 2	46. 21	47. 280	48. -120
49. -490	50. -0.3	51. -112	52. -9	53. -0.3	54. -40
55. -32	56. -0.2	57. -8	58. 16	59. -60	60. 9
61. 4	62. 7	63. -280	64. 0.4	65. 20	66. 36
67. -135	68. -21				

Page 8: Exponents

69. 1/169	70. 1/324	71. 1/3375	72. 169	73. 4,913
74. 1/361	75. 1/289	76. 6,859	77. 343	78. 1/196
79. 1/27	80. 1/512	81. 81	82. 121	83. 1/9
84. 38,416	85. 225	86. 49	87. 1/400	88. 400
89. 1	90. 27	91. 1/8	92. 1/1000	93. 1
94. 1/36	95. 1/81	96. 8,000	97. 8	98. 160,000

99. 100   100. 1/16   101. 16   102. 1,296   103. 289

104. 1/100   105. 2,744   106. 50,625   107. 625   108. 1/121

109. 361   110. 1/6859   111. 104,976   112. 1/144   113. 1,331

114. 1/2744   115. 20,736   116. 1/49

Page 12: Square and Cube Roots

117. 4   118. 2   119. 2   120. 5   121. 3   122. 18   123. 7

124. 10   125. 6   126. 7   127. 4   128. 6   129. 6   130. 20

131. 2   132. 1   133. 1   134. 97   135. 5   136. 17   137. 21

138. 26   139. 1   140. 23   141. 10   142. 3   143. 16   144. 18

145. 9   146. 8   147. 3   148. 86   149. 28   150. 9   151. 29

152. 99   153. 8   154. 93   155. 13   156. 5

Page 15: Order of Operations (PEMDAS)

157. 14   158. 403   159. 94   160. 9   161. 131   162. 73

163. 225   164. 1.8   165. 108   166. 135   167. 96   168. 86

169. 13   170. 21   171. 64   172. 94   173. 168   174. 66

175. 121   176. 32   177. 187   178. 99   179. 8   180. 144

181. 14   182. 80   183. 2.1   184. 18   185. 60   186. 70

187. 80   188. 200   189. 196   190. 20   191. 202   192. 8

193. 1.8   194. 1,301   195. 116   196. 10   197. 153   198. 126

199. 56   200. 19   201. 39   202. 15   203. 212   204. 14

205. 25   206. 80   207. 21   208. 325   209. 2   210. 200

211. 585   212. 19   213. 63   214. 24   215. 119   216. 96

217. 74   218. 8   219. 18   220. 6.5   221. 39   222. 225

223. 105   224. 12   225. 30   226. 25   227. 30   228. 28

229. 180   230. 14   231. 17   232. 1.3   233. 81   234. 88

235. 60   236. 120   237. 196   238. 80   239. 17   240. 617

241. 32   242. 25   243. -1   244. 153   245. 13   246. 73

247. 8   248. 0.9   249. 36   250. 50   251. 60   252. 30

253. 23   254. 168

Page 25: Equations (One Side)

255. $x = 16$ 256. $m = 2$ 257. $y = 19$ 258. $m = 4$ 259. $y = 10$

260. $m = 5$ 261. $x = 11$ 262. $y = 20$ 263. $y = 7$ 264. $z = 9$

265. $k = 10$ 266. $m = 15$ 267. $x = 12$ 268. $y = 8$ 269. $z = 2$

270. $m = 18$ 271. $k = 14$ 272. $m = 14$ 273. $m = 15$ 274. $k = 16$

275. $z = 13$ 276. $m = 1$ 277. $z = 17$ 278. $x = 12$ 279. $y = 7$

280. $y = 10$ 281. $z = 2$ 282. $z = 8$ 283. $z = 15$ 284. $m = 9$

285. $z = 10$ 286. $k = 13$ 287. $k = 20$ 288. $x = 3$ 289. $y = 17$

290. $m = 8$ 291. $x = 12$ 292. $x = 14$ 293. $z = 1$ 294. $k = 10$

295. $z = 6$ 296. $z = 9$ 297. $m = 17$ 298. $m = 19$ 299. $k = 12$

300. $y = 2$ 301. $y = 84$ 302. $m = 19$ 303. $x = 18$ 304. $m = 3$

305. $x = 19$ 306. $k = 1$ 307. $z = 28$ 308. $z = 15$ 309. $y = 12$

310. $m = 2$ 311. $x = 13$ 312. $m = 3$

Page 30: Equations (Two Sides)

313. $z = 9$
314. $k = 7$
315. $y = 1$
316. $k = 8$
317. $m = 4$

318. $x = 1$
319. $y = 1$
320. $z = 7$
321. $z = 8$
322. $m = 2$

323. $y = 5$
324. $z = 5$
325. $z = 6$
326. $z = 1$
327. $z = 6$

328. $m = 6$
329. $m = 7$
330. $z = 3$
331. $x = 7$
332. $k = 6$

333. $y = 8$
334. $y = 2$
335. $m = 8$
336. $y = 1$
337. $y = 8$

338. $m = 9$
339. $y = 2$
340. $m = 8$
341. $k = 8$
342. $m = 3$

343. $k = 5$
344. $y = 3$
345. $z = 6$
346. $y = 9$
347. $x = 5$

348. $y = 1$
349. $m = 3$
350. $y = 7$
351. $y = 4$
352. $y = 3$

353. $m = 5$
354. $y = 4$
355. $z = 3$
356. $k = 4$
357. $k = 6$

358. $k = 9$
359. $k = 5$
360. $x = 9$
361. $k = 7$
362. $z = 2$

363. $x = 7$
364. $m = 3$
365. $z = 2$
366. $k = 4$
367. $x = 8$

368. $k = 2$
369. $y = 9$
370. $k = 5$

Page 36: Solving Inequalities

371. $y > 5/3$
372. $y \geq -3$
373. $z > 9$
374. $m \leq 0$

375. $y < -5$
376. $m > 7$
377. $x \leq -12$
378. $z \geq 3$

379. $m < 3/2$
380. $k > 24$
381. $x < -9$
382. $z < -7$

383. $k < 6/5$
384. $y \geq 6$
385. $m < -56$
386. $y \leq -6$

387. $y > 30$
388. $z \geq -2$
389. $m \leq 5$
390. $z \geq -1$

391. $x > 40$
392. $m < -2$
393. $x \geq 11$
394. $z < 5/4$

395. $z > 3/5$
396. $x > 0$
397. $x > 1$
398. $k < 24$

399. m > 6   400. y ≤ -3/2   401. k < -1   402. k ≤ -15

403. m > 8   404. m < 5/3   405. y > -6   406. k > 14

407. x ≤ 1   408. x < 16   409. k > 5/3   410. x ≥ -8

411. y < -1   412. z ≥ 6   413. m ≥ 7   414. x > 10

415. m ≥ -5/3   416. x < 8   417. y < 1   418. y < 12

419. k > -8   420. m > -5   421. z > 48   422. z > -2/3

423. m > -8   424. k < 30   425. y > -6   426. x > 3

427. k ≥ 1/2   428. k < -2   429. x ≤ -5   430. m ≥ 45

Page 51: Solving Equations

431. 5   432. -7   433. 9   434. 8   435. 12   436. -8   437. 7   438. 1

439. 6   440. -6

Page 52: Solving Equations

441. 10   442. 11   443. 3   444. 5   445. 7   446. -5   447. 2   448. 9

449. 0   450. -6

Page 53: Solving Equations

451. 8   452. 10   453. 8   454. 6   455. 5   456. 5   457. 11   458. 7

459. 12   460. 6

Page 54: Solving Equations

461. 13   462. 12   463. 13   464. 19   465. 1.1   466. 12   467. 1   468. 15

469. 7   470. 6

Page 55: Solving Equations

471. 70   472. 3   473. 22   474. 20   475. 24   476. -2   477. 24

478. 6   479. 2   480. -8

Page 56:   Solving Equations

481. -1   482. 7   483. 1   484. -5   485. 12   486. 4   487. 5   488. 7

489. 13   490. 6

Page 57:   Solving Equations

491. -5   492. 2   493. 2   494. 21   495. 25   496. 14   497. 11   498. 1

499. 6   500. 2

Page 58:   Solving Equations

501. -5   502. 1   503. 120   504. 4   505. 32   506. 18   507. 2

508. -1   509. -4   510. 24

Page 59:   Solving Equations

511. 36   512. 13   513. 15   514. 6   515. 177   516. 33   517. 33

518. -2   519. 5   520. 0.2

Page 60:   Solving Equations

521. 1   522. 60   523. 45   524. 55   525. 62   526. 50   527. 115

528. 35   529. 6   530. 10

Page 61:   Solving Equations

531. 24   532. 10   533. 40   534. 16   535. 18   536. -3   537. 77

538. 14   539. 8   540. 12